What is this thing called Science?

WHAT IS THIS THING CALLED SCIENCE?

An assessment of the nature and status of science and its methods

SECOND EDITION

A.F. Chalmers

University of Queensland Press

©University of Queensland Press, St Lucia, Queensland 1982
First published 1976, reprinted 1978, 1979 and 1981
Second edition, 1982

Typeset by University of Queensland Press
Printed and bound by Hedges & Bell Pty Ltd, Melbourne

National Library of Australia
Cataloguing-in-Publication data

Chalmers, A.F. (Alan Francis), 1939- .
   What is this thing called science?

   2nd ed.
   Previous ed.: St. Lucia, Qld.: University of
   Queensland Press, 1976.
   Bibliography.
   Includes index.
   ISBN 0 7022 1831 6.

   1. Science — Philosophy. I. Title.
501

"Like all young men I set out to be a
genius, but mercifully laughter intervened."

Clea   Lawrence Durrell

Contents

Contents

x

Contents

Preface to the first edition

This book is intended to be a simple, clear and elementary introduction to modern views about the nature of science. When teaching philosophy of science, either to philosophy undergraduates or to scientists wishing to become familiar with recent theories about science, I have become increasingly aware that there is no suitable single book, nor even a small number of books, that one can recommend to the beginner. The only sources on the modern views that are available are the original ones. Many of these are too difficult for beginners, and in any case they are too numerous to be made easily available to a large number of students. This book will be no substitute for the original sources for anyone wishing to pursue the topic seriously, of course, but I hope it will provide a useful and easily accessible starting-point that does not otherwise exist.

My intention of keeping the discussion simple proved to be reasonably realistic for about two-thirds of the book. By the time I had reached that stage, and had begun to criticize the modern views, I found, to my surprise, first, that I disagreed with those views more than I had thought, and second, that from my criticism a fairly coherent alternative was emerging. That alternative is sketched in the latter chapters of the book. It would be pleasant for me to think that the second half of this book contains not only summaries of current views on the nature of science but also a summary of the next view.

My professional interest in history and philosophy of science began in London, in a climate that was dominated by the views of Professor Karl Popper. My debt to him, his writings, his lectures and his seminars, and also to the late Professor Imre Lakatos, must be very evident from the contents of this book. The form of the first half of it owes much to Lakatos's brilliant article on the methodology of research programmes. A noteworthy feature of the Popperian school was the pressure it put on one to be clear about the problem one was interested in and to express one's views on it in a simple and straightforward way. While I owe much to the example of Popper and Lakatos in this respect, any ability that I have to express myself simply and clearly stems mostly from my interaction with Professor Heinz Post, who was my supervisor at Chelsea College while I was working on my doctoral thesis in the Department of History and Philosophy of Science there. I cannot rid myself of an uneasy feeling that his copy of this book will be returned to me along with the demand that I rewrite the bits he does not understand. Of my colleagues in London to whom I owe a special debt, most of them students at the time, Noretta Koertge, now at Indiana University, helped me considerably.

I referred above to the Popperian school as a *school*, and yet it was not until I came to Sydney from London that I fully realized the extent to which I had been in a school. I found, to my surprise, that there were philosophers influenced by Wittgenstein or Quine or Marx who thought that Popper was quite wrong on many issues, and some who even thought that his views were positively dangerous. I think I have learnt much from that experience. One of the things that I have learnt is that on a number of major issues Popper is indeed wrong, as is argued in the latter portions of this book. However, this does not alter the fact that the Popperian approach is infinitely better than the approach adopted in most philosophy departments that I have encountered.

I owe much to my friends in Sydney who have helped to waken me from my slumber. I do not wish to imply by this that I accept their views rather than Popperian ones. They know better than that. But since I have no time for obscurantist nonsense about the incommensurability of frameworks (here Popperians prick up their ears), the extent to which I have been forced to acknowledge and counter the views of my Sydney colleagues and adversaries has led me to understand the strengths of their views and the weaknesses of my own. I hope I will not upset anyone by singling out Jean Curthoys and Wal Suchting for special mention here.

Lucky and attentive readers will detect in this book the odd metaphor stolen from Vladimir Nabokov, and will realize that I owe him some acknowledgement (or apology).

I conclude with a warm "hello" to those friends who don't care about the book, who won't read the book, and who had to put up with me while I wrote it.

Alan Chalmers,
Sydney, 1976

Preface to the second edition

Judging by responses to the first edition of this book it would seem that the first eight chapters of it function quite well as "a simple, clear and elementary introduction to modern views about the nature of science". It also seems to be fairly universally agreed that the last four chapters fail to do so. Consequently, in this revised and extended edition I have left chapters 1-8 virtually unchanged and have replaced the last four chapters by six entirely new ones. One of the problems with the latter part of the first edition was that it ceased to be simple and elementary. I have tried to keep my new chapters simple, although I fear I have not entirely succeeded when dealing with the difficult issues of the final two chapters. While I have tried to keep the discussion simple, I hope I have not thereby become uncontroversial.

Another problem with the latter part of the first edition is lack of clarity. Although I remain convinced that most of what I was groping for there was on the right track, I certainly failed to express a coherent and well-argued position, as my critics have made clear. Not all of this can be blamed on Louis Althusser, whose views were very much in vogue at the time of writing, and whose influence can still be discerned to some extent in this new edition. I have learnt my lesson and in future will be very wary of being unduly influenced by the latest Paris fashions.

My friends Terry Blake and Denise Russell have convinced me that there is more of importance in the writings of Paul Feyerabend than I was previously prepared to admit. I have given him more attention in this new edition and have tried to separate the wheat from the chaff, the anti-methodism from the dadaism. I have also been obliged to separate the important sense from "obscurantist nonsense about the incommensurability of frameworks".

The revision of this book owes much to the criticism of numerous colleagues, reviewers and correspondents. I will not attempt to name them all, but acknowledge my debt and offer my thanks.

Since the revision of this book has resulted in a new ending, the original point of the cat on the cover has been lost. However, the cat does seem to have a considerable following, despite her lack of whiskers, so we have retained her, and merely ask readers to reinterpret her grin.

Alan Chalmers,
Sydney, 1981

Introduction

In modern times, science is highly esteemed. Apparently it is a widely held belief that there is something special about science and its methods. The naming of some claim or line of reasoning or piece of research "scientific" is done in a way that is intended to imply some kind of merit or special kind of reliability. But what, if anything, is so special about science? What is this "scientific method" that allegedly leads to especially meritorious or reliable results? This book is an attempt to elucidate and answer questions of that kind.

There is an abundance of evidence from everyday life that science is held in high regard, in spite of some disenchantment with science because of consequences for which some hold it responsible, such as hydrogen bombs and pollution. Advertisements frequently assert that a particular product has been scientifically shown to be whiter, more potent, more sexually appealing or in some way preferable to rival products. By doing so, they hope to imply that their claim is particularly well-founded and perhaps beyond dispute. In a similar vein, a recent newspaper advertisement advocating Christian Science was headed, "Science speaks and says the Christian Bible is provedly true", and went on to tell us that "even the scientists themselves believe it these days". Here we have a direct appeal to the authority of science and scientists. We might well ask, "What is the basis for such authority?"

The high regard for science is not restricted to everyday life and the popular media. It is evident in the scholarly and academic world and in all parts of the knowledge industry. Many areas of study are described as sciences by their supporters, presumably in an effort to imply that the methods used are as firmly based and as potentially fruitful as in a traditional science such as physics. Political science and social science are by now commonplace. Marxists are keen to insist that historical materialism is a science. In addition, Library Science, Administrative Science, Speech Science, Forest Science, Dairy Science, Meat and Animal Science and even Mortuary Science are all currently taught or were recently taught at American colleges or universities.[1] Self-avowed "scientists" in such fields will often see themselves as following the *empirical* method of physics, which for them consists of the collection of "facts" by means of careful observation and experiment and the subsequent derivation of laws and theories from those facts by some kind of logical procedure. I was recently informed by a colleague in the history department, who apparently had absorbed this brand of empiricism, that it is not at present possible to write Australian history because we do not as yet have a sufficient number of facts. An inscription on the facade of the Social Science Research Building at the University of Chicago reads, "If you cannot measure, your knowledge is meagre and unsatisfactory".[2] No doubt, many of its inhabitants, imprisoned in their modern laboratories, scrutinize the world through the iron bars of the integers, failing to realize that the method that they endeavour to follow is not only necessarily barren and unfruitful but also is not the method to which the success of physics is to be attributed.

The mistaken view of science referred to above will be discussed and demolished in the opening chapters of this book. Even though some scientists and many pseudo-scientists voice their allegiance to that method, no modern philosopher of science would be unaware of at least some of its shortcomings. Modern developments in the philosophy of science have pinpointed and stressed deep-seated difficulties associated with the idea that science rests on a sure foundation acquired through observation and experiment and with the idea that there is some kind of inference procedure that enables us to derive scientific theories from such a base in a reliable way. There is just no method that enables scientific theories to be proven true or even probably true. Later in the book, I will argue that attempts to give a simple and straightforward logical reconstruction of the "scientific method" encounter further difficulties when it is realized that there is no method that enables scientific theories to be conclusively disproved either.

Some of the arguments to support the claim that scientific theories cannot be conclusively proved or disproved are largely based on philosophical and logical considerations. Others are based on a detailed analysis of the history of science and modern scientific theories. It has been a feature of modern developments in theories of scientific method that increasing attention has been paid to the history of science. One of the embarrassing results of this for many philosophers of science is that those episodes in the history of science that are commonly regarded as most characteristic of major advances, whether they be the innovations of Galileo, Newton, Darwin or Einstein, have not come about by anything like the methods typically described by philosophers.

One reaction to the realization that scientific theories cannot be conclusively proved or disproved and that the reconstructions of philosophers bear little resemblance to what actually goes on in science is to give up altogether the idea that science is a rational activity operating according to some special method or methods. It is a reaction somewhat like this that has recently led philosopher and entertainer Paul Feyerabend to write a book with the title *Against Method: Outline of an Anarchistic Theory of Knowledge*[3] and a paper with the title "Philosophy of Science: A Subject with a Great Past".[4] According to the most extreme view that has been read into Feyerabend's recent writings, science has no special features that render it intrinsically superior to other branches of knowledge such as ancient myths or Voodoo. A high regard for science is seen as the modern religion, playing a similar role to that played by Christianity in Europe in earlier eras. It is suggested that the choice between theories boils down to choices determined by the subjective values and wishes of individuals. This kind of response to the breakdown of traditional theories of science is resisted in this book. An attempt is made to give an account of physics that is not subjectivist or individualist, which accepts much of the thrust of Feyerabend's critique of method, but which itself is immune to that critique.

Philosophy of science has a history. Francis Bacon was one of the first to attempt to articulate what the method of modern science is. In the early seventeenth century, he proposed that the aim of science is the improvement of man's lot on earth, and for him that aim was to be achieved by collecting facts through organized observation and deriving theories from them. Since then, Bacon's theory has been modified and improved by some and challenged in a fairly radical way by others. An historical account and explanation of developments in the philosophy of science would make a very interesting study. For instance, it would be very interesting to investigate and explain the rise of *logical positivism*, which began in Vienna in the early decades of this century, became very popular and still has considerable influence today. Logical positivism was an extreme form of empiricism according to which theories are not only to be justified by the extent to which they can be verified by an appeal to facts acquired through observation, but are considered to have *meaning* only insofar as they can be so derived. There are, it seems to me, two puzzling aspects of the rise of positivism. One is that it happened at a time when, with the advent of quantum physics and Einstein's relativity theory, physics was advancing spectacularly and in a way that was very difficult to reconcile with positivism. The other puzzling aspect is that as early as 1934, Karl Popper in Vienna and Gaston Bachelard in France had both published works that contained fairly conclusive refutations of positivism, and yet this did not stem the tide of positivism. Indeed, the works of Popper and Bachelard were almost totally neglected and have only received the attention they deserve in recent times. Paradoxically, by the time A.J. Ayer introduced logical positivism to England with his book *Language, Truth and Logic*, and thus became one of the most famous English philosophers, he was preaching a doctrine some fatal shortcomings of which had already been articulated and published by Popper and Bachelard.[5]

Philosophy of science has advanced rapidly in recent decades. However, this book is not intended to be a contribution to the history of the philosophy of science. Its purpose is to catch up with recent developments by explaining as clearly and as simply as possible some modern theories about the nature of science and eventually to suggest some improvements on them. In the first half of the book, I describe two simple but inadequate accounts of science, which I refer to as inductivism and falsificationism. While the two positions that I describe do have a lot in common with positions that have been defended in the past and that are held by some even today, they are not intended primarily as historical expositions. Their main purpose is pedagogical. By understanding these extreme, somewhat caricatured positions and their faults the reader will be in a better position to understand the motivation behind the modern theories, and to appreciate their strengths and weaknesses. Inductivism is described in Chapter 1 and then severely criticized in Chapters 2 and 3. Chapters 4 and 5 are devoted to an exposition of falsificationism as an attempt to improve on inductivism, until its limitations too are dragged out into the open in Chapter 6. The next chapter expounds the sophisticated falsificationism of Imre Lakatos, and then Thomas Kuhn and his all-purpose paradigms are introduced in Chapter 8. Relativism, the idea that the worth of theories must be judged relative to the values of the individuals or groups that contemplate them, has become fashionable. In Chapter 9 this issue is raised and the extent to which Kuhn presented and Lakatos avoided a relativist position is discussed. In the following chapter I outline an approach to knowledge that I call objectivism, which in some respect is opposed to relativism. Objectivism removes individuals and their judgements from a position of primacy with respect to an analysis of knowledge. From that standpoint it becomes possible to give an account of theory change that is non-relativist in important respects, and which, nevertheless, is immune from criticism that has been levelled at traditional accounts of theory change by relativists such as Feyerabend. In Chapter 11 I present my account of theory change in physics. The stage is then set for an attempt, in Chapter 12, to come to terms with Feyerabend's case against method and the use to which he puts it. The final two chapters of the book are more difficult. They deal with the question of the extent to which our theories can be construed as a search for "true" descriptions of what the world is "really" like. In the final sections I indulge in a political sermon about the point of the book.

While the theory of science that can be extracted from the latter portion of this book is intended to be an improvement on anything that has come before, it is certainly not problem-free. It might be said that the book proceeds according to the old adage, "We start off confused and end up confused on a higher level".

1. This list is from a survey by C. Trusedell cited by J.R. Ravetz, *Scientific Knowledge and Its Social Problems* (Oxford: Oxford University Press, 1971), p. 387n.

2. T.S. Kuhn, "The Function of Measurement in Modern Physical Science", *Isis* 52 (1961): 161-93. The inscription is quoted on p.161.

3. P.K. Feyerabend, *Against Method: Outline of an Anarchistic Theory of Knowledge* (London: New Left Books, 1975).

4. P.K. Feyerabend, "Philosophy of Science: A Subject with a Great Past", in *Historical and Philosophical Perspectives of Science, Minnesota Studies in Philosophy of Science*, vol. 5, ed. Roger H. Stuewer (Minneapolis: University of Minnesota Press, 1970), pp.172-83.

5. A.J. Ayer, *Language, Truth and Logic* (London: Gollancz, 1936). I owe this point to Bryan Magee, "Karl Popper: The World's Greatest Philosopher?", *Current Affairs Bulletin* 50, no. 8 (1974): 14-23. K.R. Popper, *The Logic of Scientific Discovery* (London: Hutchinson, 1968) was first published in German in 1934. The work by Gaston Bachelard referred to in the text is *Le Nouvel Esprit Scientifique* (Paris: Presses Universitaires de France, 1934).

1

Inductivism: Science as Knowledge Derived from the Facts of Experience

1. A widely held common-sense view of science

Scientific knowledge is proven knowledge. Scientific theories are derived in some rigorous way from the facts of experience acquired by observation and experiment. Science is based on what we can see and hear and touch, etc. Personal opinion or preferences and speculative imaginings have no place in science. Science is objective. Scientific knowledge is reliable knowledge because it is objectively proven knowledge.

I suggest that statements of the foregoing kind sum up what in modern times is a popular view of the kind of thing that scientific knowledge is. This view first became popular during and as a consequence of the Scientific Revolution that took place mainly during the seventeenth century and that was brought about by such great pioneering scientists as Galileo and Newton. The philosopher Francis Bacon and many of his contemporaries summed up the scientific attitude of the times when they insisted that if we want to understand nature we must consult nature and not the writings of Aristotle. The progressive forces of the seventeenth century came to see as mistaken the preoccupation of mediaeval natural philosophers with the works of the ancients, especially Aristotle, and also with the Bible, as the sources of scientific knowledge. Spurred on by the successes of "great experimenters" like Galileo, they came more and more to regard experience as the source of knowledge. This assessment has only been enhanced since then by the spectacular achievements of experimental science. "Science is a structure built upon facts", writes J.J. Davies in his book *On The Scientific Method.*[1] And here is a modern assessment of Galileo's achievement, due to H.D. Anthony:

It was not so much the observations and experiments which Galileo made that caused the break with tradition as his *attitude* to them. For him, the facts based on them were treated as facts, and not related to some preconceived idea. . . . The facts of observation might, or might not, fit into an acknowledged scheme of the universe, but the important thing, in Galileo's opinion, was to accept the facts and build the theory to fit them.[2]

The *naive inductivist* account of science, which I will outline in the following sections, can be looked on as an attempt to formalize this popular picture of science. I have called it *inductivist* because it is based on inductive reasoning, as will be explained shortly. In later chapters, I will argue that this view of science, together with the popular account that it resembles, is quite mistaken and even dangerously misleading. I hope that by then it will be apparent why the adjective "naive" is appropriate for the description of many inductivists.

2. Naive inductivism

According to the naive inductivist, science starts with observation. The scientific observer should have normal, unimpaired sense organs and should faithfully record what he can see, hear, etc. to be the case with respect to the situation he is observing, and he should do this with an unprejudiced mind. Statements about the state of the world, or some part of it, can be justified or established as true in a direct way by an unprejudiced observer's use of his senses. The statements so arrived at (I will call them observation statements) then form the basis from which the laws and theories that make up scientific knowledge are to be derived. Here are some examples of some not very exciting observation statements.

At twelve midnight on 1 January 1975, Mars appeared at such and such a position in the sky.

That stick, partially immersed in water, appears bent.

Mr Smith struck his wife.

The litmus paper turned red when immersed in the liquid.

The truth of such statements is to be established by careful observation. Any observer can establish or check their truth by direct use of his or her senses. Observers can see for themselves.

Statements of the kind cited above fall in the class of so-called *singular statements.* Singular statements, unlike a second class of statements that we will meet shortly, refer to a particular occurrence or state of affairs at a particular place at a particular time. The first statement refers to a particular appearance of Mars at a particular place in the sky at a specified time, the second to a particular observation of a particular stick, and so on. It is clear that all observation statements will be singular statements. They result from an observer's use of his or her senses at a particular place and time.

Next, we look at some simple examples that might form part of scientific knowledge.

From astronomy: Planets move in ellipses around their sun.

From physics: When a ray of light passes from one medium to another, it changes direction in such a way that the sine of the angle of incidence divided by the sine of the angle of refraction is a constant characteristic of the pair of media.

From psychololgy: Animals in general have an inherent need for some kind of aggressive outlet.

From chemistry: Acids turn litmus red.

These are general statements that make claims about the properties or behaviour of some aspect of the universe. Unlike singular statements, they refer to *all* events of a particular kind at all places and at all times. All planets, wherever they are situated, always move in ellipses around their sun. Whenever refraction takes place it always takes place according to the law of refraction stated above. The laws and theories that make up scientific knowledge all make general assertions of that kind, and such statements are called *universal statements.*

The following question can now be posed. If science is based on experience, then by what means is it possible to get from the singular statements that result from observation to the universal statements that make up scientific knowledge? How can the very general, unrestricted claims that constitute our theories be justified on the basis of limited evidence comprised of a limited number of observation statements?

The inductivist answer is that, provided certain conditions are satisfied, it is legitimate to *generalize* from a finite list of singular observation statements to a universal law. For instance, it may be legitimate to generalize from a finite list of observation statements referring to litmus paper turning red on being immersed in acid to the universal law, "Acids turn litmus red", or to generalize from a list of observations referring to heated metals to the law, "Metals expand when heated". The conditions that must be satisfied for such generalizations to be considered legitimate by the inductivist can be listed thus:

1. The number of observation statements forming the basis of a generalization must be large.

2. The observations must be repeated under a wide variety of conditions.

3. No accepted observation statement should conflict with the derived universal law.

Condition (1) is regarded as necessary because it is clearly not legitimate to conclude that all metals expand when heated on the basis of just one observation of a metal bar's expansion, say, any more than it is legitimate to conclude that all Australians are drunkards on the basis of one observation of an intoxicated Australian. A large number of independent observations will be necessary before either generalization can be justified. The inductivist insists that we should not jump to conclusions.

One way of increasing the number of observations in the examples mentioned would be to repeatedly heat a single bar of metal, or to continually observe a particular Australian getting drunk night after night, and perhaps morning after morning. Clearly, a list of observation statements acquired in such a way would form a very unsatisfactory basis for the respective generalizations. That is why condition (2) is necessary. "All metals expand when heated" will only be a legitimate generalization if the observations of expansion on which it is based range over a wide variety of conditions. Various kinds of metals should be heated, long iron bars, short iron bars, silver bars, copper bars, etc. should be heated at high pressure and low pressure, high temperatures and low temperatures, and so on. If, on all such occasions, the heated samples of metal all expand, then and only then is it legitimate to generalize from the resulting list of observation statements to the general law. Further, it is evident that if a particular sample of metal is observed not to expand when heated, then the universal generalization will not be justified. Condition (3) is essential.

The kind of reasoning that we have discussed, which takes us from a finite list of singular statements to the justification of a universal statement, which takes us from some to all, is called *inductive* reasoning and the process is called induction. We might sum up the naive inductivist position by saying that, according to it, science is based on the *principle of induction*, which we can write:

> If a large number of As have been observed under a wide variety of conditions, and if all those observed As without exception possessed the property B, then all As have the property B.

According to the naive inductivist, then, the body of scientific knowledge is built by induction from the secure basis provided by observation. As the number of facts established by observation and experiment grows, and as the facts become more refined and esoteric due to improvements in our observational and experimental skills, so more and more laws and theories of ever more generality and scope are constructed by careful inductive reasoning. The growth of science is continuous, ever onward and upward, as the fund of observational data is increased.

The analysis so far constitutes only a partial account of science. For surely a major feature of science is its ability to *explain* and *predict*. It is scientific knowledge that enables an astronomer to predict when the next eclipse of the sun will occur or a physicist to explain why the boiling-point of water is lower than normal at high altitudes. Figure 1 depicts, in schematic form, a summary of the complete inductivist story of science. The left-handed side of the figure refers to the derivation of scientific laws and theories from observation that we have already discussed. It remains to discuss the right-hand side. Before doing so, a little will be said of the character of logic and deductive reasoning.

3. Logic and deductive reasoning

Once a scientist has universal laws and theories at his disposal, it is possible for him to derive from them various consequences that serve as explanations and predictions. For instance, given the fact that metals expand when heated, it is possible to derive the fact that continuous railway tracks not interrupted by small gaps will become distorted in the hot sun. The kind of reasoning involved in derivations of this kind is called *deductive* reasoning. Deduction is distinct from the induction discussed in the previous section.

A study of deductive reasoning constitutes the discipline of

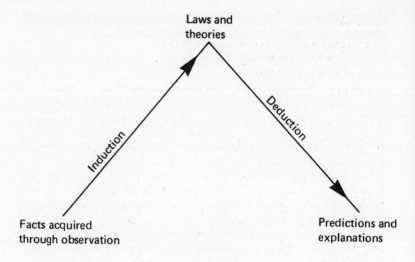

Figure 1

logic.[3] No attempt will be made to give a detailed account and appraisal of logic here. Rather, some of its important features relevant to our analysis of science will be illustrated by means of trivial examples.

Here is an example of a logical deduction.

Example 1:

1. All books on philosophy are boring.
2. This book is a book on philosophy.
3. This book is boring.

In this argument, (1) and (2) are the premises and (3) is the conclusion. It is self-evident, I take it, that if (1) and (2) are true, then (3) is bound to be true. It is not possible for (3) to be false once it is given that (1) and (2) are true. For (1) and (2) to be true and (3) to be false would involve a contradiction. This is the key feature of a *logically valid* deduction. If the premises of a logically valid deduction are true, then the conclusion must be true.

A slight modification of the above example will give us an instance of a deduction that is not valid.

Example 2:

1. Many books on philosophy are boring.
2. This book is a book on philosophy.
3. This book is boring.

In this example, (3) does not follow of necessity from (1) and (2). It is possible for (1) and (2) to be true and yet for (3) to be false. Even if (1) and (2) are true, then this book may yet turn out to be one of the minority of books on philosophy that is not boring. Asserting (1) and (2) as true and (3) as false does not involve a contradiction. The argument is invalid.

The reader may by now be feeling bored. Experiences of that kind certainly have a bearing on the truth of statements (1) and (3), in examples (1) and (2). But a point that needs to be stressed here is that logic and deduction alone cannot establish the truth of factual statements of the kind figuring in our examples. All that logic can offer in this connection is that *if* the premises are true *then* the conclusion must be true. But whether the premises are true or not is not a question that can be settled by an appeal to logic. An argument can be a perfectly logical deduction even if it involves a premise that is in fact false. Here is an example.

Example 3:

1. All cats have five legs.
2. Bugs Pussy is my cat.
3. Bugs Pussy has five legs.

This is a perfectly valid deduction. It is the case that if (1) and (2) are true, then (3) must be true. It so happens that in this example, (1) and (3) are false. But this does not affect the status of the argument as a valid deduction. Deductive logic alone, then, does not act as a source of true statements about the world. Deduction is concerned with the derivation of statements from other given statements.

4. Prediction and explanation in the inductivist account

We are now in a position to understand in a simple way the functioning of laws and theories as predictive and explanatory devices in science. Once again, I will start with a trivial example to illustrate the point. Consider the following argument:

What is this thing called Science?

1. Fairly pure water freezes at about 0°C (if given sufficient time).
2. My car radiator contains fairly pure water.
3. If the temperature falls below 0°C, the water in my car radiator will freeze (if given sufficient time).

Here we have an example of a valid logical argument to deduce the prediction (3) from the scientific knowledge contained in premise (1). If (1) and (2) are true, (3) must be true. However, the truth of (1), (2) or (3) is not established by this or any other deduction. For an inductivist, the source of truth is not logic but experience. On that view, (1) will be ascertained by direct observation of freezing water. Once (1) and (2) have been established by observation and induction then the prediction (3) can be *deduced* from them.

Less trivial examples will be more complicated, but the roles played by observation, induction and deduction remain essentially the same. As a final example, I will consider the inductivist account of how physical science is able to explain the rainbow.

The simple premise (1) of the previous example is here replaced by a number of laws governing the behaviour of light, namely the laws of reflection and refraction of light and assertions about the dependence of the degree of refraction on colour. These general principles are derived from experience by induction. A large number of laboratory experiments are performed, reflecting rays of light from mirrors and water surfaces, measuring angles of incidence and refraction for rays of light passing from air to water, water to air, etc., under a wide variety of conditions, repeating the experiments with light of various colours, and so on, until the conditions that need to be met to legitimate the inductive generalization to the laws of optics are satisfied.

Premise (2) of the previous example will also be replaced by a more complex array of statements. These will include assertions to the effect that the sun is situated at some specified position in the sky with respect to an observer on earth, and that raindrops are falling from a cloud situated in some specified region relative to the observer. Sets of statements like these, which describe the details of the set-up under investigation, will be referred to as *initial conditions*. Descriptions of experimental set-ups will be typical examples of initial conditions.

Given the laws of optics and the initial conditions, it is now possible to perform deductions yielding an explanation of the formation of a rainbow visible to the observer. These deductions will no longer be as self-evident as in our previous examples and will involve mathematical as well as verbal arguments. The argument will run roughly as follows. If we assume a raindrop to be roughly spherical, then the path of a ray of light through a raindrop will be roughly as depicted in Figure 2. If a ray of white light is incident on a raindrop at *a*, then, if the law of refraction is true, the red ray will travel along *ab*, and the blue ray will travel along *ab'*. Again, if the laws governing reflection are true, then *ab*, must be reflected along *bc*, and *ab'* along *b'c'*. Refraction at *c* and *c'* will again be determined by the law of refraction, so that an observer viewing the raindrop will see the red and blue components of the white light separated (and also all the other colours of the spectrum). The same separation of colours will also be made visible to our observer for any raindrop that is situated in a region of the sky such that the line joining the raindrop to the sun makes an angle *D* with the line joining the raindrop to the observer. Geometrical considerations then yield the conclusion that a coloured arc will be visible to the observer provided the rain cloud is sufficiently extended.

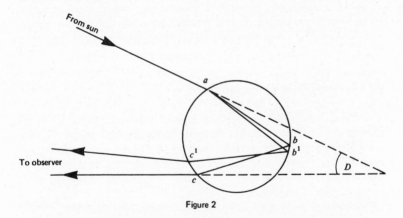

Figure 2

I have only sketched the explanation of the rainbow here, but what is offered should suffice to illustrate the general form of the reasoning involving. Given that the laws of optics are true (and for the naive inductivist, this can be established from observation by induction), and given that the initial conditions are accurately described, then the explanation of the rainbow necessarily follows. The general form of all scientific explanations and predictions can be summarized thus:

1. Laws and theories
2. Initial conditions
3. Predictions and explanations

This is the step depicted on the right-hand side of Figure 1.

The following description of the scientific method by a twentieth-century economist conforms closely to the naive inductivist account of science as I have described it, and indicates that it is not a position that I have invented solely for the purpose of criticizing it.

If we try to imagine how a mind of superhuman power and reach, but normal so far as the logical processes of its thought are concerned, . . . would use the scientific method, the process would be as follows: First, all facts would be observed and recorded, *without selection* or *a priori* guess as to their relative importance. Secondly, the observed and recorded facts would be analysed, compared, and classified, without *hypothesis or postulates*, other than those necessarily involved in the logic of thought. Third, from this analysis of the facts, generalizations would be inductively drawn as to the relations, classificatory or casual, between them. Fourth, further research would be deductive as well as inductive, employing inferences from previously established generalizations.[4]

5. The appeal of naive inductivism

The naive inductivist account of science does have some apparent merits. Its attraction would seem to lie in the fact that it gives a formalized account of some of the popularly held impressions concerning the character of science, its explanatory and predictive power, its objectivity and its superior reliability compared with other forms of knowledge.

We have already seen how the naive inductivist accounts for the explanatory and predictive power of science.

The objectivity of inductivist science derives from the fact that both observation and inductive reasoning are themselves objective. Observation statements can be ascertained by any observer by normal use of the senses. No personal, subjective elements should be permitted to intrude. The validity of the observation statements when correctly acquired will not depend on the taste, opinion, hopes or expectations of the observer. The same goes for the inductive reasoning by means of which scientific knowledge is derived from the observation statements. Either the inductions satisfy the prescribed conditions or they do not. It is not a subjective matter of opinion.

The reliability of science follows from the inductivist's claims about observation and induction. The observation statements that form the basis of science are secure and reliable because their truth can be ascertained by direct use of the senses. Further, the reliability of observation statements will be transmitted to the laws and theories derived from them, provided the conditions for legitimate inductions are satisfied. This is guaranteed by the principle of induction that forms the basis of science according to the naive inductivist.

I have already mentioned that I regard the naive inductivist account of science to be very wrong and dangerously misleading. In the next two chapters, I will begin to say why. However, I should perhaps make it clear that the position I have outlined is a very extreme form of inductivism. Many more sophisticated inductivists would not wish to be associated with some of the characteristics of my naive inductivism. Nevertheless, all inductivists would claim that in so far as scientific theories can be justified, they are justified by supporting them inductively on the basis of some more-or-less secure basis provided by experience. Subsequent chapters of this book will provide us with plenty of reasons for doubting that claim.

FURTHER READING

The naive inductivism that I have described is too naive to be sympathetically dealt with by philosophers. One of the classic, more sophisticated attempts to systematize inductive reasoning is John Stuart Mill's *A System of Logic* (London: Longman, 1961). An excellent, simple summary of more modern views is Wesley C. Salmon, *The Foundations of Scientific Inference* (Pittsburgh: Pittsburgh University Press, 1975). The extent to which inductivist philosophers are concerned with the empirical basis of knowledge and its origin in sense perception is very evident in A.J. Ayer, *The Foundations of Empirical Knowledge* (London: Macmillan, 1955). A good simple description and discussion of the traditional positions on sense perception is C.W.K. Mundle, *Perception: Facts and Theories* (Oxford: Oxford University Press, 1971). For a taste of that particular brand of inductivism referred to as logical positivism, I suggest two collections, A.J. Ayer, ed., *Logical Positivism* (Glencoe: Free Press, 1959) and P.A. Schilpp, ed., *The*

Philosophy of Rudolf Carnap (La Salle, Illinois: Open Court, 1963). The extent to which the inductivist programme became a highly technical one is evident in R. Carnap, *Logical Foundations of Probability* (Chicago: University of Chicago Press, 1962).

1. J.J. Davies, *On the Scientific Method* (London: Longman, 1968), p.8.
2. H.D. Anthony, *Science and Its Background* (London: Macmillan, 1948), p.145.
3. Logic is sometimes taken to include the study of inductive reasoning, so that there is an inductive logic as well as a deductive logic. In this book, logic is understood to be the study of deductive reasoning only.
4. This quotation, due to A.B. Wolfe, is as cited by Carl G. Hempel, *Philosophy of Natural Science* (Englewood Cliffs, N.J.: Prentice-Hall, 1966), p.11. The italics are in the original quotation.

2

The Problem of Induction

1. Can the principle of induction be justified?

According to the naive inductivist, science starts with observation, observation supplies a secure basis upon which scientific knowledge can be built, and scientific knowledge is derived from observation statements by induction. In this chapter, the inductivist account of science will be criticized by casting doubt on the third of these assumptions. Doubt will be cast on the validity and justifiability of the principle of induction. Afterwards, in Chapter 3, the first two assumptions will be challenged and refuted.

My rendering of the principle of induction reads: "If a large number of As have been observed under a wide variety of conditions, and if all those observed As without exception have possessed the property B, then all As possess the property B". This principle, or something very much like it, is the basic principle on which science is founded, if the naive inductivist position is accepted. In the light of this, an obvious question with which to confront the inductivist is, "How can the principle of induction be justified?" That is, if observation provides us with a secure set of observation statements as our starting-point (an assumption that we have granted for the sake of the argument of this chapter), why is it that *inductive* reasoning leads to reliable and perhaps even true scientific knowledge? There are two lines of approach open to the inductivist in attempting to answer this question. He might try to justify the principle by appealing to logic, a recourse that we freely grant him, or he might attempt to justify the principle by appealing to experience, a recourse that lies at the basis of his whole approach to science. Let us examine these two lines of approach in turn.

Valid logical arguments are characterized by the fact that, if the premise of the argument is true, then the conclusion must be true. Deductive arguments possess that character. The principle of induction would certainly be justified if inductive arguments also possessed it. But they do not. Inductive arguments are not logically valid arguments. It is not the case that, if the premises of an inductive inference are true, then the conclusion must be true. It is possible for the conclusion of an inductive argument to be false and for the premises to be true and yet for no contradiction to be involved. Suppose, for example, that up until today I have observed a large number of ravens under a wide variety of circumstances and have observed all of them to have been black and that, on that basis, I conclude, "All ravens are black". This is a perfectly legitimate inductive inference. The premises of the inference are a large number of statements of the kind, "Raven x was observed to be black at time t", and all these we take to be true. But there is no logical guarantee that the next raven I observe will not be pink. If this proved to be the case, then "All ravens are black" would be false. That is, the initial inductive inference, which was legitimate insofar as it satisfied the criteria specified by the principle of induction, would have led to a false conclusion, in spite of the fact that all premises of the inference were true. No logical contradiction is involved in claiming that all observed ravens have proved to be black and also that not all ravens are black. Induction cannot be justified purely on logical grounds.

A more interesting if rather gruesome example of the point is an elaboration of Bertrand Russell's story of the inductivist turkey. This turkey found that, on his first morning at the turkey farm, he was fed at 9 a.m. However, being a good inductivist, he did not jump to conclusions. He waited until he had collected a large number of observations of the fact that he was fed at 9 a.m., and he made these observations under a wide variety of circumstances, on Wednesdays and Thursdays, on warm days and cold days, on rainy days and dry days. Each day, he added another observation statement to his list. Finally, his inductivist conscience was satisfied and he carried out an inductive inference to conclude, "I am always fed at 9 a.m.". Alas, this conclusion was shown to be false in no uncertain manner when, on Christmas eve, instead of being fed, he had his throat cut. An inductive inference with true premises has led to a false conclusion.

The principle of induction cannot be justified merely by an appeal to logic. Given this result, it would seem that the inductivist, according to his own standpoint, is now obliged to indicate how the principle of induction can be derived from experience. What would such a derivation be like? Presumably, it would go something like this. Induction has been observed to work on a large number of occasions. For example, the laws of optics, derived by induction from the results of laboratory experiments, have been used on numerous occasions in the design of optical instruments and these instruments have functioned satisfactorily. Again, the laws of planetary motion, derived from observations of planetary positions etc., have been successfully employed to predict the occurrence of eclipses. This list could be greatly extended with accounts of successful predictions and explanations made possible by inductively derived scientific laws and theories. In this way, the principle of induction is justified.

The foregoing justification of induction is quite unacceptable, as David Hume conclusively demonstrated as long ago as the mid-eighteenth century. The argument purporting to justify induction is circular because it employs the very kind of inductive argument the validity of which is supposed to be in need of justification. The form of the justificatory argument is as follows:

> The principle of induction worked successfully on occasion x_1.
> The principle of induction worked successfully on occasion x_2 etc.
> The principle of induction always works.

A universal statement asserting the validity of the principle of induction is here inferred from a number of singular statements recording past successful applications of the principle. The argument is therefore an inductive one and so cannot be used to justify the principle of induction. We cannot use induction to justify induction. This difficulty associated with the justification of induction has traditionally been called "the problem of induction".

It would seem, then, that the unrepentant naive inductivist is in trouble. The extreme demand that all knowledge should be derived from experience by induction rules out the principle of induction basic to the inductivist position.

In adition to the circularity involved in attempts to justify the principle of induction, the principle as I have stated it suffers from other shortcomings. These shortcomings stem from the vagueness and dubiousness of the demand that a "large number" of observations be made under a "wide variety" of circumstances.

How many observations make up a large number? Should a metal bar be heated ten times, a hundred times, or how many times before we can conclude that it always expands when heated?

Whatever the answer to such a question, examples can be produced that cast doubt on the invariable necessity for a large number of observations. To illustrate this, I refer to the strong public reaction against nuclear warfare that followed the dropping of the first atomic bomb on Hiroshima towards the end of the second world war. This reaction was based on the understanding that atomic bombs cause widespread death and destruction and extreme human suffering. And yet this generally held belief was based on just one dramatic observation. Again, it would take a very stubborn inductivist to put his hand in a fire many times before concluding that fire burns. In circumstances like these, the demand for a large number of observations seem inappropriate. In other situations, the demand seems more plausible. For instance, we would be justifiably reluctant to ascribe supernatural powers to a fortune-teller on the basis of just one correct prediction. Nor would it be justifiable to conclude some causal connection between smoking and lung cancer on the evidence of just one heavy smoker contracting the disease. It is clear, I think, from these examples that if the principle of induction is to be a guide to what counts as a legitimate scientific inference, then the "large number" clause will need to be qualified in some detail.

The naive inductivist position is further threatened when the demand that observations be made under a wide variety of circumstances is scrutinized. What is to count as a significant variation in the circumstances? When investigating the boiling-point of water, for instance, is it necessary to vary the pressure, the purity of the water, the method of heating and the time of day? The answer to the first two suggestions is "Yes" and to the second two it is "No". But what are the grounds for these answers? This question is important because the list of variations can be extended indefinitely by adding a variety of further variations such as the colour of the container, the identity of the experimenter, the geographical location, and so on. Unless such "superfluous" variations can be eliminated, the number of observations necessary to render an inductive inference legitimate will be infinitely large. What, then, are the grounds on which a large number of variations are deemed superfluous? I suggest the answer is clear enough. The variations that are significant are distinguished from those that are superfluous by appealing to our *theoretical knowledge of the situation* and of the kinds of physical mechanisms operative. But, to admit this is to admit that theory plays a vital role *prior to* observation. The naive inductivist cannot afford to make such an admission. However, to pursue this would lead on to criticisms of inductivism that I have reserved for the next chapter. Here I merely note that the "wide variety of circumstances" clause in the principle of induction poses serious problems for the inductivist.

2. The retreat to probability

There is a fairly obvious way in which the extreme naive inductivist position criticized in the previous section can be weakened in an attempt to counter some of the criticism. An argument in defence of a weaker position might run somewhat as follows.

We cannot be one hundred per cent sure that, just because we have observed the sun to set each day on many occasions, the sun will set every day. (Indeed, in the Arctic and Antarctic, there are days when the sun does not set.) We cannot be one hundred per cent sure that the next dropped stone will not "fall" upwards. Nevertheless, although generalizations arrived at by legitimate inductions cannot be guaranteed to be perfectly true, they are *probably* true. In the light of the evidence, it is very probable that the sun will always set in Sydney, and that stones will fall downwards when they are dropped. Scientific knowledge is not proven knowledge, but it does represent knowledge that is probably true. The greater the number of observations forming the basis of an induction and the greater variety of conditions under which these observations are made, the greater the probability that the resulting generalizations are true.

If this modified version of induction is adopted, then the principle of induction will be replaced by a probabilistic version that will read something like, "If a large number of *A*s have been observed under a wide variety of conditions, and if all these observed *A*s without exception have possessed the property *B*, then all *A*s probably possess the property *B*". This reformulation does not overcome the problem of induction. The reformulated principle is still a universal statement. It implies, on the basis of a finite number of successes, that all applications of the principle will lead to general conclusions that are probably true. Attempts to justify the probabilistic version of the principle of induction by appeal to experience must suffer from the same deficiency as attempts to justify the principle in its original form. The justification will employ an argument of the very kind that is seen as in need of justification.

Even if the principle of induction in its probabilistic version could be justified, there are further problems facing our more cautious inductivist. The further problems are associated with difficulties that are encountered when trying to be precise about just how probable a law or theory is in the light of specified evidence. It may seem intuitively plausible that as the observational support that a universal law receives increases, the probability that it is true also increases. But this intuition does not stand up to inspection. Given standard probability theory, it is very difficult to construct an account of induction that avoids the consequence that the probability of any universal statement making claims about the world is zero, whatever the observational evidence. To make the point in a non-technical way, any observational evidence will consist of a finite number of observation statements, whereas a universal statement makes claims about an infinite number of possible situations. The probability of the universal generalization being true is thus a finite number divided by an infinite number, which remains zero however much the finite number of observation statements constituting the evidence is increased.

This problem, associated with attempts to ascribe probabilities to scientific laws and theories in the light of given evidence, has given rise to a detailed technical research programme that has been tenacioulsy pursued and developed by inductivists over the last few decades. Artificial languages have been constructed for which it is possible to ascribe unique, non-zero probabilities to generalizations, but the languages are so restricted that they contain no universal generalizations. They are far removed from the language of science.

Another attempt to save the inductivist programme involves giving up the idea of ascribing probabilities to scientific laws and theories. Instead, attention is directed towards the probability of individual predictions being correct. According to this approach, the object of science is, for instance, to gauge the probability of the sun rising tomorrow rather than the probability that it will always rise. Science is expected to be able to provide a guarantee that a bridge of some design will withstand various stresses and not collapse, but not that all bridges of that design will be satisfactory. Some systems have been developed along such lines that enable non-zero probabilities to be ascribed to individual predictions. Two criticisms of them will be mentioned here. Firstly, the notion that science is concerned with the production of a set of individual predictions rather than with the production of *knowledge* in the form of a complex of general statements is, to say the least, counter-intuitive. Secondly, even when attention is restricted to individual predictions, it can be argued that scientific theories, and hence universal statements, are inevitably involved in the estimation of the likelihood of a prediction being successful. For instance, in some intuitive, non-technical sense of "probable", we may be prepared to assert that it is to some degree probable that a very heavy smoker will die of lung cancer. The evidence supporting the assertion would presumably be the available statistical data. But this intuitive probability will be significantly increased if there is a plausible and well-supported theory available that entails some causal connection between smoking and lung cancer. Similarly, estimates of the probability that the sun will rise tomorrow will be increased once the knowledge of the laws governing the behaviour of the solar system are taken into account. But this dependence of the probability of the correctness of predictions on universal laws and theories undermines the attempt of the inductivists to ascribe non-zero probabilities to individual predictions. Once universal statements are involved in a significant way, the probabilities of the correctness of individual predictions again threaten to be zero.

3. Possible responses to the problem of induction

Faced with the problem of induction and related problems, inductivists have run into one difficulty after another in their attempts to construe science as a set of statements that can be established as true or probably true in the light of given evidence. Each manoeuvre in their rearguard action has taken them further away from intuitive notions about that exciting enterprise referred to as science. Their technical programme has led to interesting advances within probability theory, but it has not yielded new insights into the nature of science. Their programme has degenerated.

There are a number of possible responses to the problem of induction. One of them is a sceptical one. We can accept that science is based on induction and Hume's demonstration that induction cannot be justified by appeal to logic or experience, and conclude that science cannot be rationally justified. Hume himself adopted a position of that kind. He held that beliefs in laws and theories are nothing more than psychological habits that we acquire as a result of repetitions of the relevant observations.

A second response is to weaken the inductivist demand that all non-logical knowledge must be derived from experience and to argue for the reasonableness of the principle of induction on some other grounds. However, to regard the principle of induction, or something like it as "obvious" is not acceptable. What we regard as obvious is much too dependent on and relative to our education, our prejudices and our culture to be a reliable guide to what is reasonable. To many cultures, at various stages in history, it was obvious that the earth was flat. Before the scientific revolution of Galileo and Newton, it was obvious that if an object was to move, then it required a force or cause of some kind to make it move. This may be obvious to some readers of this book lacking a physics education, and yet it is false. If the principle of induction is to be defended as reasonable, then some more sophisticated argument than an appeal to its obviousness must be offered.

A third response to the problem of induction involves the denial that science is based on induction. The problem of induction will be avoided if it can be established that science does not involve induction. The falsificationists, most notably Karl Popper, attempt to do this. We will discuss those attempts in some detail in Chapters 4, 5 and 6.

In this chapter, I have sounded much too much like a philosopher. In the next chapter, I move on to a more interesting, more telling and more fruitful critique of inductivism.

FURTHER READING

The historical source of Hume's problem of induction is Part 3 of D. Hume, *Treatise on Human Nature* (London: Dent, 1939). Another classic discussion of the problem is Chapter 6 of B. Russell, *Problems of Philosophy* (Oxford: Oxford University Press, 1912). A very thorough and technical investigation and discussion of the consequences of Hume's argument by an inductivist sympathizer is D.C. Stove, *Probability and Hume's Inductive Scepticism* (Oxford: Oxford University Press, 1973). Popper's claim to have solved the problem of induction is summarized In K.R. Popper, "Conjectural Knowledge: My Solution to the Problem of Induction", in his *Objective Knowledge* (Oxford: Oxford University Press, 1972), Ch. 1. A criticism of Popper's position from the point of view of a falsificationist sympathizer is I. Lakatos, "Popper on Demarcation and Induction", in *The Philosophy of Karl R. Popper*, ed. P.A. Schlipp (La Salle, Illinois: Open Court, 1974), pp. 241-73. Lakatos has written a provocative history of developments in the inductivist programme in his "Changes in the Problem of Inductive Logic", in *The Problem of Inductive*

Logic, ed. I. Lakatos (Amsterdam: North Holland Publ. Co., 1968), pp. 315-417. Criticisms of inductivism from a point of view somewhat different from the one adopted in this book are in the classic P. Duhem, *The Aim and Structure of Physical Theory* (New York: Atheneum, 1962).

3

The Theory-Dependence
of Observation

We have seen that, according to our naive inductivist, careful and unprejudiced observation yields a secure basis from which probably true, if not true, scientific knowledge can be derived. In the last chapter, this position was criticized by pointing to difficulties involved in any attempt to justify the inductive reasoning involved in the derivation of scientific laws and theories from observation. Some examples suggested that there are positive grounds for suspecting the alleged reliability of inductive reasoning. Nevertheless, these arguments do not constitute a definitive refutation of inductivism, especially as it turns out that many rival theories of science face a similar, related difficulty.[1] In this chapter, a more serious objection to the inductivist's position is developed that involves a criticism, not of the inductions by which scientific knowledge is supposed to be derived from observation, but of the inductivist's assumptions concerning the status and role of observation itself.

There are two important assumptions involved in the naive inductivist position with respect to observation. One is that *science starts with observation*. The other is that *observation yields a secure basis* from which knowledge can be derived. In the present chapter, both of these assumptions will be criticized in a variety of ways and rejected for a variety of reasons. But first of all, I will sketch an account of observation that I think it is fair to say is a commonly held one in modern times, and which lends plausibility to the naive inductivist position.

1. A popular account of observation

Partly because the sense of sight is the sense most extensively used in the practice of science, and partly for convenience, I will restrict my discussion of observation to the realm of seeing. In most cases, it will not be difficult to see how the argument presented could be re-cast so as to be applicable to observation via the other senses. A simple, popular account of seeing might run as follows. Humans see by using their eyes. The most important components of the human eye are a lens and a retina, the latter acting like a screen on which images of objects external to the eye are formed. Rays of light from a viewed object pass from the object to the lens via the intervening medium. These rays are refracted by the material of the lens in such a way that they are brought to a focus on the retina, so forming an image of the viewed object. Thus far, the functioning of the eye is very much like that of a camera. A big difference lies in the way the final image is recorded. Optic nerves pass from the retina to the central cortex of the brain. These carry information concerning the light falling on the various regions of the retina. It is the recording of this information by the human brain that corresponds to the seeing of the object by the human observer. Of course, many details could be added to this simple description, but the account offered does capture the general idea.

Two points are strongly suggested by the foregoing sketch of observation via the sense of sight, points that are key ones for the inductivist. The first is that a human observer has more or less direct access to some properties of the external world insofar as those properties are recorded by the brain in the act of seeing. The second is that two normal observers viewing the same object or scene from the same place will "see" the same thing. An identical combination of light rays will strike the eye of each observer, will be focused on their normal retinas by their normal eye lenses and give rise to similar images. Similar information will then travel to the brain of each observer via their normal optic nerves, resulting in the two observers "seeing" the same thing. These two points will be attacked fairly directly in the next section. Later sections will cast further and more consequential doubt on the adequacy of the inductivist stance on observation.

2. Visual experiences not determined by the images on the retina

There is a vast fund of evidence to indicate that it is just not the case that the experience that observers undergo when viewing an object is determined solely by the information, in the form of light rays, entering the observer's eyes, nor is it determined solely by the images on the retinas of an observer. Two normal observers viewing the same object from the same place under the same physical circumstances do not necessarily have identical visual experiences, even though the images on their respective retinas may be virtually identical. There is an important sense in which the two observers need not "see" the same thing. As N.R. Hanson has put it, "There is more to seeing than meets the eyeball". Some simple examples will illustrate the point.

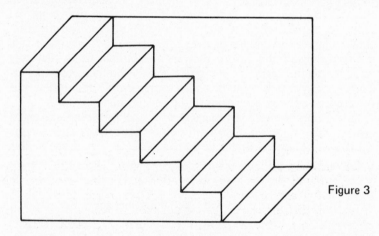

Figure 3

Most of us, when first looking at Figure 3, see the drawing of a staircase with the upper surface of the stairs visible. But this is not the only way it can be seen. It can without difficulty also be seen as a staircase with the under surface of the stairs visible. Further, if one looks at the picture for some time, one generally finds, involuntarily, that what one sees changes frequently from a staircse viewed from above to a staircse viewed from below and back again. And yet it seems reasonable to suppose that, since it remains the same object viewed by the observer, the retinal images do not change. Whether the picture is seen as a staircase viewed from above or a staircase viewed from below seems to depend on something other than the image on the retina of the viewer. I suspect that no reader of this book has questioned my claim that Figure 3 looks like a staircase of some kind. However, the results of experiments on members of a number of African tribes whose culture does not include the custom of depicting three-dimensional objects by two-dimensional perspective drawings indicate that the members of those tribes would not have seen Figure 3 as a staircase but as a two-dimensional array of lines. I presume that the nature of the images formed on the retinas of observers is relatively independent of their culture. Again, it seems to follow that the perceptual experiences that observers have in the act of seeing is not uniquely determined by the images on their retinas. This point has been made and illustrated with a number of examples by Hanson.[2]

What an observer sees, that is, the visual experience that an observer has when viewing an object, depends in part on his past experience, his knowledge and his expectations. Here are two simple examples to illustrate this particular point.

In a well-known experiment, subjects were shown playing-cards for a small duration of time and asked to identify them. When a normal pack of cards was employed, subjects were able to accomplish this task very successfully. But when anomalous cards were introduced, such as a red Ace of Spades, then, at first, nearly all subjects initially identified such cards incorrectly as some normal card. They saw a red Ace of Spades as a normal Ace of Diamonds or a normal Ace of Spades. The subjective impressions experienced by the observers were influenced by their expectations. When, after a period of confusion, subjects began to realize, or were told, that there were anomalous cards among the pack; they then had no trouble correctly identifying all the cards shown to them, anomalous or otherwise. The change in their knowledge and expectations was accompanied by a change in what they saw, although they were still viewing the same physical objects.

Another example is provided by a children's picture puzzle that involves finding the drawing of a human face amongst the foliage in the drawing of a tree. Here, what is seen, that is, the subjective impression experienced by a person viewing the drawing, at first corresponds to a tree, with trunk, leaves, branches. But this changes once the human face has been detected. What was once seen as foliage and parts of branches is now seen as a human face. Again, the same physical object has been viewed before and after the solution of the puzzle, and presumably the image on the observer's retina does not change at the moment the solution is found and the face discovered. And if the picture is viewed at some later time, the face can be easily seen again by an observer who has already solved the puzzle once. In this example, what an observer sees is affected by his knowledge and experience.

"What", it might be suggested, "have these contrived examples got to do with science?" In response, it is not difficult to produce examples from the practice of science that illustrate the same point, namely, that what observers see, the subjective experiences that they undergo, when viewing an object or scene is not determined solely by the images on their retinas but depends also on the experience, knowledge, expectations and general inner state of the observer. It is necessary to learn how to see expertly through a telescope or microscope, and the unstructured array of bright and dark patches that the beginner observes is different from the detailed specimen or scene that the skilled viewer can discern. Something of the kind must have been operative when Galileo first introduced the telescope as an instrument for exploring the heavens. The reservations that Galileo's rivals held about accepting phenomena such as the moons of Jupiter that Galileo had learnt to see must have been in part due, not to prejudice, but to genuine difficulties encountered when learning to "see" through what were, after all, very crude telescopes. In the following passage, Michael Polanyi describes the changes in a medical student's perceptual experience when he is taught to make a diagnosis by inspecting an X-ray picture.

Think of a medical student attending a course in the X-ray diagnosis of pulmonary diseases. He watches, in a darkened room, shadowy traces on a fluorescent screen placed against a patient's chest, and hears the radiologist commenting to his assistants, in technical language, on the significant features of these shadows. At first, the student is completely puzzled. For he can see in the X-ray picture of a chest only the shadows of the heart and ribs, with a few spidery blotches between them. The experts seem to be romancing about figments of their imagination; he can see nothing that they are talking about. Then, as he goes on listening for a few weeks, looking carefully at ever-new pictures of different cases, a tentative understanding will dawn on him; he will gradually forget about the ribs and begin to see the lungs. And eventually, if he perseveres intelligently, a rich panorama of significant details will be revealed to him: of physiological variations and pathological changes, of scars, of chronic infections and signs of acute disease. He has entered a new world. He still sees only a fraction of what the experts can see, but the pictures are definitely making sense now and so do most of the comments made on them.[3]

A common response to the claim that I am making about observation, supported by the kinds of examples I have utilized, is that observers viewing the same scene from the same place see the same thing but interpret what they see differently. I wish to dispute this. As far as perception is concerned, the only thing with which an observer has direct and immediate contact are his or her experiences. These experiences are not uniquely given and unchanging but vary with the expectations and knowledge of the observer. What is uniquely given by the physical situation is the image on the retina of an observer, but an observer does not have direct perceptual contact with that image. When the naive inductivist, and many other empiricists, assume that there is something unique given to us in experience that can be interpreted in various ways, they are assuming, without argument and in spite of much evidence to the contrary, some one-to-one correspondence between the images on our retinas and the subjective experiences that we have when seeing. They are taking the camera analogy too far.

Having said this, let me try to make clear what I do *not* mean to be claiming in this section, lest I be taken to be arguing for more than I intend to be. Firstly, I am certainly not claiming that the physical causes of the images on our retinas have nothing to do with what we see. We cannot see just what we like. However, while the images on our retinas form part of the cause of what we see, another very important part of the cause is constituted by the inner state of our minds or brains, which will clearly depend on our cultural upbringing, our knowledge, our expectations, etc. and will not be determined solely by the physical properties of our eyes and the scene observed. Secondly, under a wide variety of circumstances, what we see in various situations remains fairly stable. The dependence of what we see on the state of our minds or brains is not so sensitive as to make communication, and science, impossible. Thirdly, in all the examples quoted here, there is a sense in which all observers see the same thing. I accept, and presuppose throughout this book, that a single, unique, physical world exists independently of observers. Hence, when a number of observers look at a picture, a piece of apparatus, a microscope slide, or whatever, there is a sense in which they are all confronted by, look at, and so, in a sense, "see" the same thing. But it does not follow from this that they have identical perceptual experiences. There is a very important sense in which they do not see the same thing, and it is this latter sense upon which my criticism of the inductivist position has been based.

3. Observation statements presuppose theory

Even if there were some unique experience given to all observers in perception, there still remain some major objections to the inductivist assumption concerning observations. In this section, we focus attention on the observation *statements* based on and allegedly justified by the perceptual experiences of the observers who assert the statements. According to the inductivist account of science, the secure basis on which the laws and theories that constitute science are built is made up of public observation statements rather than the private, subjective experiences of individual observers. Clearly, the observations made by Darwin during his voyage on the *Beagle*, for example, would have been inconsequential for science had they remained Darwin's private experiences. They became relevant for science only when they were formulated and communicated as observation statements capable of being utilized and criticized by other scientists. The inductivist account requires the derivation of universal *statements* from singular *statements* by induction. Inductive as well as deductive reasoning involves the relationships between various sets of statements and not relationships between statements on the one hand and perceptual experiences on the other.

We might assume that perceptual experiences of some kind are directly accessible to an observer, but observation statements certainly are not. The latter are public entities, formulated in a public language, involving theories of various degrees of generality and sophistication. Once attention is focused on observation statements as forming the alleged secure basis for science, it can be seen that, contrary to the inductivists' claim, theory of some kind must precede all observation statements and observation statements are as fallible as the theories they presuppose.

Observation statements must be made in the language of some theory, however vague. Consider the simple sentence in commonsense language, "Look out, the wind is blowing the baby's pram over the cliff edge!" Much low-level theory is presupposed here. It is implied that there is such a thing as wind, which has the property of being able to cause the motion of objects such as prams, which stand in its path. The sense of urgency conveyed by the "Look out" indicates the expectation that the pram, complete with baby, will fall over the cliff and perhaps be dashed on the rocks beneath and it is further assumed that this will be deleterious for the baby. Again, when an early riser in urgent need of coffee complains, "The gas won't light", it is assumed that there are substances in the world that can be grouped under the concept "gas", and that some of them, at least, ignite. It is also to the point to note that the concept "gas" has not always been available. It did not exist until the mid-eighteenth century, when Joseph Black first prepared carbon dioxide. Before that, all "gases" were considered to be more or less pure samples of air.[4] When we move towards statements of the kind occuring in science, the theoretical presuppositions become less commonplace and more obvious. That there is considerable theory presupposed by the assertion, "The electron beam was repelled by the North Pole of the magnet", or by a psychiatrist's talk of the withdrawal symptoms of a patient, should not need much arguing.

Observation statements, then, are always made in the language of some theory and will be as precise as the theoretical or conceptual framework that they utilize is precise. The concept "force" as used in physics is precise because it acquires its meaning from the role it plays in a precise, relatively autonomous theory, Newtonian mechanics. The use of the same word in everyday language (the force of circumstance, gale-force-winds, the force of an argument, etc.) is imprecise just because the corresponding theories are multifarious and imprecise. Precise, clearly formulated theories are a prerequisite for precise observation statements. In this sense theories precede observation.

The foregoing claims about the priority of theory over observation run counter to an inductivist thesis that the meanings of many basic concepts are acquired through observation. Let us consider the simple concept "red" as an example. An inductivist account might run roughly as follows. From all the perceptual experiences of an observer arising from the sense of sight, a certain set of them (those corresponding to the perceptual experiences arising from sightings of red objects) will have something in common. The observer, by inspection of the set, is somehow able to discern the common element in these perceptions, and come to understand this common element as redness. In this way, the concept "red" is arrived at through observation. This account contains a serious flaw. It assumes that from all the infinity of perceptual experiences undergone by an observer, the set of perceptual experiences arising from the viewing of red things is somehow available for inspection. But that set does not select itself. What is the criterion according to which some perceptual experiences are included in the set and others are excluded? The criterion, of course, is that only perceptions of *red* objects are included in the set. The account presupposes the very concept, redness, the acquisition of which it is meant to explain. It is not an adequate defence of the inductivist position to point out that parents and teachers select a set of red objects when teaching children to understand the concept "red", for we are interested in how the concept first acquired its meaning. The claim that the concept "red" or any other concept is derived from experience and from nothing else is false.

So far in this section the naive inductivist account of science has been undermined largely by arguing that theories must precede observation statements, so that it is false to claim that science starts with observation. We now come to a second way in which inductivism is undermined. Observation statements are as fallible as the theories they presuppose and therefore do not constitute a completely secure basis on which to build scientific laws and theories.

I will first illustrate the point with some simple, somewhat contrived examples, and then proceed to indicate the relevance of the point for science by citing some examples from science and its history.

Consider the statement, "Here is a piece of chalk", uttered by a teacher as he indicates a cylindrical white stick held in front of the blackboard. Even this most basic of observation statements involves theory, and is fallible. Some very low-level generalization, such as "White sticks found in classrooms near blackboards are pieces of chalk", is assumed. And, of course, this generalization need not be true. The teacher in our example may be wrong. The white cylinder in question may not be a piece of chalk but a carefully contrived fake placed there by a scheming pupil in search of amusement. The teacher, or anyone else present, could take steps to test the truth of the statement, "Here is a piece of chalk", but it is significant that the more stringent the test the more theory is called upon, and further, absolute certainty is never attained. For instance, on being challenged, the teacher might draw the white cylinder across the board, point to the resulting white trace and declare, "There you are, it *is* a piece of chalk". This involves the assumption, "Chalk leaves white traces when drawn across a blackboard". The teacher's demonstration might be countered by the retort that other things besides chalk leave white traces on a blackboard. Perhaps, after other moves by the teacher, such as crumbling the chalk, being countered in a similar way, the determined teacher might resort to chemical analysis. Chemically, chalk is largely calcium carbonate, he argues, and so should yield carbon dioxide if immersed in an acid. He performs the test and demonstrates that the evolving gas is carbon dioxide by showing that it turns lime water milky. Each stage in this series of attempts to consolidate the validity of the observation statement, "Here is a piece of chalk", involves an appeal not only to further observation statements but also to more theoretical generalizations. The test that formed the stopping-point in our series involved a certain amount of chemical theory (the effect of acids on carbonates, the peculiar effect of carbon dioxide on lime water). In order to establish the validity of an observation statement, then, it is necessary to appeal to theory, and the more firmly the validity is to be established, the more extensive will be the theoretical knowledge employed. This is in direct contrast to what we might expect to follow according to the inductivist view, namely, that in order to establish the truth of some problematic observation statement we appeal to more secure observation statements, and perhaps laws derived inductively from them, but not to theory.

In everyday language, it is often the case that an apparently unproblematic "observation statement" is found to be false when an expectation is disappointed, due to the falsity of some theory presupposed in the assertion of the observation statement. For instance, some picnickers at the top of a high mountain, directing their glance towards the camp-fire, may observe, "The water is hot enough to make the tea", and then find they were sadly wrong when tasting the resulting brew. The theory that had wrongly been supposed is that boiling water is hot enough to make tea. This need not be the case for water boiling under the low pressures experienced at high altitudes.

Here are some less-contrived examples more helpful for our attempt to understand the nature of science.

At the time of Copernicus (before the invention of the telescope), careful observations were made of the size of Venus. The statement, "Venus, as viewed from earth, does not change size appreciably during the course of the year", was generally accepted by all astronomers, both Copernicans and non-Copernicans, on the basis of those observations. Andreas Osiander, a contemporary of Copernicus, referred to the prediction that Venus should appear to change size during the year as "a result contradicted by the experience of every age".[5] The observation was accepted in spite of its inconvenience, since the Copernican theory as well as some of its rivals predicted that Venus should appear to change size appreciably during the course of the year. Yet the statement is now considered to be false. It presupposes the false theory that the size of small light sources is accurately gauged by the naked eye. Modern theory can offer some explanation of why naked-eye estimates of the size of small light sources will be misleading and why telescopic observations, which show the apparent size of Venus to vary considerably during the course of the year, are to be preferred. This example clearly illustrates the theory dependence and hence fallibility of observation statements.

A second example concerns electrostatics. Early experimenters in that field reported observations of electrified rods becoming sticky, as evidenced by small pieces of paper sticking to them, and of the rebounding of one electrified body from another. From a modern point of view, those observation reports were mistaken. The false conceptions that facilitated those observations would now be replaced by the notions of attractive and repulsive forces acting at a distance, leading to quite different observation reports.

Finally, in lighter vein, modern scientists would have no difficulty in exposing the falsity of an entry in honest Kepler's notebook, following observations through a Galilean, telescope, which reads, "Mars is square and intensely coloured".[6]

In this section, I have argued that the inductivist is wrong on two counts. Science does not start with observation statements because theory of some kind precedes all observation statements, and observation statements do not constitute a firm basis on which scientific knowledge can be founded because they are fallible. However, I do not wish to claim that it follows from this that observation statements should play no role in science. I am not urging that all observation statements should be discarded because they are fallible. I am merely arguing that the role in science attributed to observation statements by the inductivist is incorrect.

4. Observation and experiment are guided by theory

According to the most naive of inductivists, the basis of scientific knowledge is provided by observations made by an unprejudiced and unbiased observer.[7] If interpreted anything like literally, this position is absurd and untenable. To illustrate this, let us imagine

Heinrich Hertz, in 1888, performing the electrical experiment that enabled him to produce and detect radio waves for the first time. If he is to be totally unbiased when making his observations, then he will be obliged to record not only the readings on various meters, the presence or absence of sparks at various critical locations in the electrical circuits, the dimensions of the circuit etc. but also the colour of the meters, the dimensions of the laboratory, the state of the weather, the size of his shoes and a whole host of "clearly irrelevant" details, irrelevant, that is, to the kind of theory in which Hertz was interested and which he was testing. (In this particular case Hertz was testing Maxwell's electromagnetic theory to see if he could produce the radio waves predicted by that theory.) As a second, hypothetical example, suppose that I was keen to make some contribution to human physiology or anatomy, and suppose I noted that very little work has been done on the weight of human earlobes. If, on the basis of this, I were to proceed to make very careful observations of the weights of a wide variety of human earlobes, recording and categorizing the many observations, I think it is clear that I would not be making any significant contribution to science. I would be wasting my time, unless some theory had been proposed rendering the weight of earlobes important, such as a theory connecting the size of earlobes with the incidence of cancer in some way.

The foregoing examples illustrate an important sense in which theory precedes observation in science. Observations and experiments are carried out in order to test or shed light on some theory, and only those observations considered relevant to that task should be recorded. However, insofar as the theories that make up our scientific knowledge are fallible and incomplete, the guidance that theories offer as to what observations are relevant to some phenomenon under investigation may be misleading, and may result in some important factors being overlooked. Hertz's experiment referred to above provides a nice example. One of the factors I referred to as "clearly irrelevant" was in fact very relevant. It was a consequence of the theory under test that radio waves should have a velocity equal to the velocity of light. When Hertz measured the velocity of his radio waves, he found repeatedly that their velocity was significantly different from that of light. He was never able to solve the problem. It was not until after his death that the source of the problem was really understood. Radio waves emitted from his apparatus were being reflected from the walls of his laboratory back on to the apparatus and were interfering with his measurements. It turned out that the dimensions of the laboratory were very relevant. The fallible and incomplete theories that make up scientific knowledge may give false guidance to an observer, then. But this problem is to be tackled by improving and extending our theories and not by recording an endless list of aimless observations.

5. Inductivism not conclusively refuted

The theory-dependence of observation discussed in this chapter certainly undermines the inductivist claim that science starts with observation. However, only the most naive of inductivists would wish to adhere to that position. None of the modern, more sophisticated inductivists would wish to uphold the literal version of it. They can dispense with the claim that science must start with unbiased and unprejudiced observation by making a distinction between the way a theory is first thought of or discovered on the one hand, and the way in which it is justified or its merits assessed on the other. According to this modified position, it is freely admitted that new theories are conceived of in a variety of ways and often by a number of routes. They may occur to the discoverer in a flash of inspiration, as in the mythical story of Newton's discovery of the law of gravitation being triggered by his seeing an apple fall from a tree. Alternatively, a new discovery might occur as the result of an accident, as Roentgen was led to the discovery of X-rays by the constant blackening of photographic plates stored in the vicinity of his discharge tube. Or, again, a new discovery might be arrived at after a long series of observations and calculations, as exemplified by Kepler's discoveries of his laws of planetary motion. Theories may be, and usually are, conceived of prior to the making of those observations necessary to test them. Further, according to this more sophisticated inductivism, creative acts, the most novel and significant of which require genius and involving as they do the psychology of individual scientists, defy logical analysis. Discovery and the question of the origin of new theories is excluded from the philosophy of science.

However, once new laws and theories have been arrived at, no matter by what route, there remains the question of the adequacy of those laws and theories. Do they correspond to legitimate scientific knowledge or don't they? This question is the concern of the sophisticated inductivists. Their answer is roughly as I have outlined in Chapter 1. A large number of facts relevant to a theory must be ascertained by observation under a wide variety of circumstances, and the extent to which the theory can be shown to be true or probably true in the light of those facts by some kind of inductive inference must be established.

The separation of the mode of discovery and the mode of justification does enable the inductivists to evade that part of the criticism levelled at them in this chapter which was directed at the claim that science starts with observation. However, the legitimacy of the separation of the two modes can be questioned. For instance, it would surely seem reasonable to suggest that a theory that anticipates and leads to the discovery of new phenomena, in the way Clerk Maxwell's theory led to the discovery of radio waves, is more worthy of merit and more justifiable than a law or theory devised to account for phenomena already known and not leading to the discovery of new ones. It will, I hope, become increasingly clear as this book progresses that it is essential to understand science as an historically evolving body of knowledge and that a theory can only be adequately appraised if due attention is paid to its historical context. Theory appraisal is intimately linked with the circumstances under which a theory first makes its appearance.

Even if we allow the inductivists to separate the mode of discovery and the mode of justification, their position is still threatened by the fact that observation statements are theory-laden and hence fallible. The inductivist wishes to make a fairly sharp distinction between direct observation, which he hopes will form a secure foundation for scientific knowledge, and theories, which are to be justified by the extent to which they receive inductive support from the secure observational foundation. Those extreme inductivists, the logical positivists, went so far as to say that theories only have meaning insofar as they can be verified by direct observation. This position is undermined by the fact that the sharp distinction between observation and theory cannot be maintained because observation, or rather the statements resulting from observation, are permeated by theory.

Although I have severely criticized inductivist philosophies of science in this and the previous chapter, the arguments I have presented do not constitute an absolutely decisive refutation of that programme. The problem of induction cannot be regarded as a decisive refutation because, as I have previously mentioned, most other philosophies of science suffer from a similar difficulty. I have just indicated one way in which criticism centred on the theory dependence of observation can be to some extent evaded by the inductivists, and I am convinced that they will be able to think of further ingenious defences. The main reason why I think inductivism should be abandoned is that, compared with rival and more modern approaches, it has increasingly failed to throw new and interesting light on the nature of science, a fact that led Imre Lakatos to describe the programme as a degenerating one. The increasingly more adequate, more interesting and more fruitful accounts of science developed in later chapters will constitute the strongest case against inductivism.

FURTHER READING

The dependence of perceptual experiences on theory is discussed and illustrated with examples in N.R. Hanson, *Patterns of Discovery* (Cambridge: Cambridge University Press, 1958). The writings of Popper, Feyerabend and Kuhn abound with arguments and examples supporting the thesis that observations and observation statements are theory-dependent. Some passages dealing fairly specifically with the topic are K.R. Popper, *The Logic of Scientific Discovery* (London: Hutchinson, 1968), Ch. 5 and Appendix *10; Popper, *Objective Knowledge* (Oxford: Oxford University Press, 1972), pp.341-61; Feyerabend, *Against Method: Outline of an Anarchistic Theory of Knowledge* (London: New Left Books, 1975), Ch. 6 and 7; and T.S. Kuhn, *The Structure of Scientific Revolutions* (Chicago: Chicago University Press, 1970), Ch. 10. Chapter 1 of Carl R. Kordig, *The Justification of Scientific Change* (Dordrecht: Reidel Publ. Co., 1971) contains a discussion of the topic which is critical of Hanson and Feyerabend. A circumspect but somewhat dry account is Israel Scheffler, *Science and Subjectivity* (New York: Bobbs-Merrill, 1967). Entertaining discussions of perception that are relevant to the philosophical issue are R.L. Gregory, *Eye and Brain* (London: Weidenfeld and Nicolson, 1972) and Ernst Gombrich, *Art and Illusion* (New York: Pantheon, 1960). I would also like to enthusiastically recommend a very exciting book on animal perception, Vitus B. Droscher, *The Magic of the Senses* (New York: Harper and Row, 1971). This book strongly conveys a sense of the limitations and restrictedness of human perception and the arbitrariness of attempts to attach fundamental significance to the information humans happen to receive through their senses.

1. See Chapter 12, section 4.
2. N.R. Hanson, *Patterns of Discovery* (Cambridge: Cambridge University Press, 1958), Ch. 1.

3. M. Polanyi, *Personal Knowledge* (London: Routledge and Kegan Paul, 1973), p.101.
4. See T.S. Kuhn, *The Structure of Scientific Revolutions* (Chicago: University of Chicago Press, 1970), p.70.
5. E. Rosen, *Three Copernican Treatises* (New York: Dover, 1959), p.25.
6. P.K. Feyeraband, *Against Method: Outline of an Anarchistic Theory of Knowledge* (London: New Left Books, 1975), p.126.
7. See, for example, the quotation on p.9.

4

Introducing Falsificationism

The falsificationist freely admits that observation is guided by and presupposes theory. He is also happy to abandon any claim implying that theories can be established as true or probably true in the light of observational evidence. Theories are construed as speculative and tentative conjectures or guesses freely created by the human intellect in an attempt to overcome problems encountered by previous theories and to give an adequate account of the behaviour of some aspects of the world or universe. Once proposed, speculative theories are to be rigorously and ruthlessly tested by observation and experiment. Theories that fail to stand up to observational and experimental tests must be eliminated and replaced by further speculative conjectures. Science progresses by trial and error, by conjectures and refutations. Only the fittest theories survive. While it can never be legitimately said of a theory that it is true, it can hopefully be said that it is the best available, that it is better than anything that has come before.

1. A logical point to support the falsificationist

According to falsificationism, some theories can be shown to be false by an appeal to the results of observation and experiment. There is a simple, logical point that seems to support the falsificationist here. I have already indicated in Chapter 2 that, even if we assume that true observational statements are available to us in some way, it is never possible to arrive at universal laws and theories by logical deductions on that basis alone. On the other hand, it is possible to perform logical deductions starting from singular observation statements as premises, to arrive at the falsity of universal laws and theories by logical deduction. For example, if we are given the statement, "A raven which was not black, was observed at place x at time t", then it logically follows from this that "All ravens are black" is false. That is, the argument

Premise   A raven, which was not black, was observed at place x at time t.

Conclusion Not all ravens are black.

is a logically valid deduction. If the premise is asserted and the conclusion denied, a contradiction is involved. One or two more examples will help illustrate this fairly trivial logical point. If it can be established by observation in some test experiment that a 10 lb. weight and a 1 lb. weight in free fall move downwards at roughly the same speed, then it can be concluded that the claim that bodies fall at speeds proportional to their weight is false. If it can be demonstrated beyond doubt that a ray of light passing close to the sun is deflected in a curved path, then it is not the case that light necessarily travels in straight lines.

The falsity of universal statements can be deduced from suitable singular statements. The falsificationist exploits this logical point to the full.

2. Falsifiability as a criterion for theories

The falsificationist sees science as a set of hypotheses that are tentatively proposed with the aim of accurately describing or accounting for the behaviour of some aspect of the world or universe. However, not any hypothesis will do. There is one fundamental condition that any hypothesis or system of hypotheses must satisfy if it is to be granted the status of a scientific law or theory. If it is to form part of science, an hypothesis must be *falsifiable*. Before proceeding any further, it is important to be clear about the falsificationist's usage of the term "falsifiable".

Here are some examples of some simple assertions that are falsifiable in the sense intended.

1. It never rains on Wednesdays.
2. All substances expand when heated.
3. Heavy objects, such as a brick when released near the surface of the earth, fall straight downwards if not impeded.
4. When a ray of light is reflected from a plane mirror, the angle of incidence is equal to the angle of reflection.

Assertion (1) is falsifiable because it can be falsified by observing rain to fall on a Wednesday. Assertion (2) is falsifiable. It can be falsified by an observation statement to the effect that some substance, *x*, did not expand when heated at time *t*. Water near its freezing-point would serve to falsify (2). Both (1) and (2) are falsifiable and false. Assertions (3) and (4) may be true, for all I know. Nevertheless, they are falsifiable in the sense intended. It is logically possible that the next brick to be relased will "fall" upwards. No logical contradiction is involved in the assertion, "The brick fell upwards when released", although it may be that no such statement is ever supported by observation. Assertion (4) is falsifiable because a ray of light incident on a mirror at some oblique angle could conceivably be reflected in a direction perpendicular to the mirror. This will never happen if the law of reflection happens to be true, but no logical contradiction would be involved if it did. Both (3) and (4) are falsifiable, even though they may be true.

An hypothesis is falsifiable if there exists a logically possible observation statement or set of observation statements that are inconsistent with it, that is, which, if established as true, would falsify the hypothesis.

Here are some examples of statements that do not satisfy this requirement and that are consequently not falsifiable.

5. Either it is raining or it is not raining.
6. All points on a Euclidean circle are equidistant from the centre.
7. Luck is possible in sporting speculation.

No logically possible observation statement could refute (5). It is true whatever the weather is like. Assertion (6) is necessarily true because of the definition of a Euclidean circle. If points on a circle were not equidistant from some fixed point, then that figure would just not be a Euclidean circle. "All bachelors are unmarried" is unfalsifiable for a similar reason. Assertion (7) is quoted from a horoscope in a newspaper. It typifies the fortune-teller's devious strategy. The assertion is unfalsifiable. It amounts to telling the reader that if he has a bet today, he might win, which remains true whether he bets or not, and if he does, whether he wins or not.

The falsificationist demands that scientific hypotheses be falsifiable, in the sense I have discussed. He insists on this because it is only by ruling out a set of logically possible observation statements that a law or theory is informative. If a statement is unfalsifiable, then the world can have any properties whatsoever, can behave in any way whatsoever, without conflicting with the statement. Statements (5), (6) and (7), unlikes statements (1), (2), (3) and (4), tell us nothing about the world. A scientific law or theory should ideally give us some information about how the world does in fact behave, thereby ruling out ways in which it could (logically) possibly behave but in fact does not. The law, "All planets move in ellipses around the sun", is scientific because it claims that planets in fact move in ellipses and rules out orbits that are square or oval. Just because the law makes definite claims about planetary orbits, it has informative content and is falsifiable.

A cursory glance at some laws that might be regarded as typical components of scientific theories indicates that they satisfy the falsifiability criterion. "Unlike magnetic poles attract each other", "An acid added to a base yields a salt plus water" and similar laws can easily be construed as falsifiable. However, the falsificationist maintains that some theories, while they may superficially appear to have the characteristics of good scientific theories, are in fact only posing as scientific theories because they are not falsifiable and should be rejected. Popper has claimed that some versions at least of Marx's theory of history, Freudian psychoanalysis and Adlerian psychology suffer from this fault. The point can be illustrated by the following caricature of Adlerian psychology.

A fundamental tenet of Adler's theory is that human actions are motivated by feelings of inferiority of some kind. In our caricature, this is supported by the following incident. A man is standing on the bank of a treacherous river at the instant a child falls into the river, nearby. The man will either leap into the river in an attempt to save the child or he will not. If he does leap in, the Adlerian responds by indicating how this supports his theory. The man obviously needed to overcome his feeling of inferiority by demonstrating that he was brave enough to leap into the river, in spite of the danger. If the man does not leap in, the Adlerian can again claim support for his theory. The man was overcoming his feelings of inferiority by demonstrating that he had the strength of will to remain on the bank, unperturbed, while the child drowned.

If this caricature is typical of the way in which Adlerian theory operates, then the theory is not falsifiable.[1] It is consistent with any kind of human behaviour, and just because of that, it tells us nothing about human behaviour. Of course, before Adler's theory can be rejected on these grounds, it would be necessary to investigate the details of the theory rather than a caricature. But there are plenty of social, psychological and religious theories that give rise to the suspicion that, in their concern to explain everything, they explain nothing. The existence of a loving God and the occurrence of some disaster can be made compatible by interpreting the disaster as being sent to try us or to punish us, whichever seems most suited to the situation. Many examples of animal behaviour can be seen as evidence supporting the assertion, "Animals are designed so as best to fulfil the function for which they were intended". Theorists operating in this way are guilty of the fortune-teller's evasion and are subject to the falsificationist's criticism. If a theory is to have informative content, it must run the risk of being falsified.

3. Degree of falsifiability, clarity and precision

A good scientific law or theory is falsifiable just because it makes definite claims about the world. For the falsificationist, it follows fairly readily from this that the more falsifiable a theory is the better, in some loose sense of more. The more a theory claims, the more potential opportunities there will be for showing that the world does not in fact behave in the way laid down by the theory. A very good theory will be one that makes very wide-ranging claims about the world, and which is consequently highly falsifiable, and is one that resists falsification whenever it is put to the test.

The point can be illustrated by means of a trivial example. Consider the two laws:

(a) Mars moves in an ellipse around the sun.
(b) All planets move in ellipses around their sun.

I take it that it is clear that (b) has a higher status than (a) as a piece of scientific knowledge. Law (b) tells us all that (a) tells us and more besides. Law (b), the preferable law, is more falsifiable than (a). If observations of Mars should turn out to falsify (a), then they would falsify (b) also. Any falsification of (a) will be a falsification of (b), but the reverse is not the case. Observation statements referring to the orbits of Venus, Jupiter, etc. that might conceivably falsify (b) are irrelevant to (a). If we follow Popper and refer to those sets of observation statements that would serve to falsify a law or theory as *potential falsifiers* of that law or theory, then we can say that the potential falsifiers of (a) form a class that is a subclass of the potential falsifiers of (b). Law (b) is more falsifiable than law (a), which is tantamount to saying that it claims more, that it is the better law.

A less-contrived example involves the relation between Kepler's theory of the solar system and Newton's. Kepler's theory I take to be his three laws of planetary motion. Potential falsifiers of that theory consist of sets of statements referring to planetary positions relative to the sun at specified times. Newton's theory, a better theory that superseded Kepler's, is more comprehensive. It consists of Newton's laws of motion plus his law of gravitation, the latter asserting that all pairs of bodies in the universe attract each other with a force that varies inversely as the square of their separation. Some of the potential falsifiers of Newton's theory are sets of statements of planetary positions at specified times. But there are many others, including those referring to the behaviour of falling bodies and pendulums, the correlation between the tides and the locations of the sun and moon, and so on. There are many more opportunities for falsifying Newton's theory than for falsifying Kepler's theory. And yet, so the falsificationist story goes, Newton's theory was able to resist attempted falsifications, thereby establishing its superiority over Kepler's.

Highly falsifiable theories should be preferred to less falsifiable ones, then, provided they have not in fact been falsified. The qualification is important for the falsificationist. Theories that have been falsified must be ruthlessly rejected. The enterprise of science consists in the proposal of highly falsifiable hypotheses, followed by deliberate and tenacious attempts to falsify them. To quote Popper:

> I can therefore gladly admit that falsificationists like myself much prefer an attempt to solve an interesting problem by a bold conjecture, *even (and especially) if it soon turns out to be false,* to any recital of a sequence of irrelevant truisms. We prefer this because we believe that this is the way in which we can learn from our mistakes; and that in finding that our conjecture was false we shall have learnt much about the truth, and shall have got nearer to the truth.[2]

We learn from our *mistakes*. Science progresses by trial and *error*. Because of the logical situation that renders the derivation of universal laws and theories from observation statements impossible, but the deduction of their falsity possible, *falsifications* become the important landmarks, the striking achievements, the major growing-points in science. This somewhat counter-intuitive emphasis of the more extreme falsificationists on the significance of falsifications will be criticized in later chapters.

Because science aims at theories with a large informative content, the falsificationist welcomes the proposal of bold speculative conjectures. Rash speculations are to be encouraged, provided they are falsifiable and provided they are rejected when falsified. This do-or-die attitude clashes with the caution advocated by the naive inductivist. According to the latter, only those theories that can be shown to be true or probably true are to be admitted into science. We should proceed beyond the immediate results of experience only so far as legitimate inductions will take us. The falsificationist, by contrast, recognizes the limitation of induction and the subservience of observation to theory. Nature's secrets can only be revealed with the aid of ingenious and penetrating theories. The greater the number of conjectured theories that are confronted by the realities of the world, and the more speculative those conjectures are, the greater will be the chances of major advances in science. There is no danger in the proliferation of speculative theories because any that are inadequate as descriptions of the world can be ruthlessly eliminated as the result of observational or other tests.

The demand that theories should be highly falsifiable has the attractive consequence that theories should be clearly stated and precise. If a theory is so vaguely stated that it is not clear exactly what it is claiming, then, when tested by observation or experiment it can always be interpreted so as to be consistent with the results of those tests. In this way, it can be defended against falsifications. For example, Goethe wrote of electricity that

> it is a nothing, a zero, a mere point, which, however, dwells in all apparent existences, and at the same time is the point of origin whence, on the slightest stimulus, a double appearance presents itself, an appearance which only manifests itself to vanish. The conditions under which this manifestation is excited are infinitely varied, according to the nature of particular bodies.[3]

If we take this quotation at face value, it is very difficult to see what possible set of physical circumstances could serve to falsify it. Just because it is so vague and indefinite (at least when taken out of context), it is unfalsifiable. Politicians and fortune-tellers can avoid being accused of making mistakes by making their assertions so vague that they can always be construed as compatible with whatever may eventuate. The demand for a high degree of falsifiability rules out such manoeuvres. The falsificationist demands that theories be stated with sufficient clarity to run the risk of falsification.

A similar situation exists with respect to precision. The more precisely a theory is formulated the more falsifiable it becomes. If we accept that the more falsifiable a theory is the better (provided it has not been falsified), then we must also accept that the more precise the claims of a theory are the better. "Planets move in ellipses around the sun" is more precise than "Planets move in closed loops around the sun", and is consequently more falsifiable. An oval orbit would falsify the first but not the second, whereas any orbit that falsifies the second will also falsify the first. The falsificationist is committed to preferring the first. Similarly, the falsificationist must prefer the claim that the velocity of light in a vacuum is 299.8×10^6 metres per second to the less-precise claim that it is about 300×10^6 metres per second, just because the first is more falsifiable than the second.

The closely associated demands for precision and clarity of expression both follow naturally from the falsificationist's account of science.

4. Falsificationism and progress

The progress of science as the falsificationist sees it might be summed up as follows. Science starts with problems, problems associated with the explanation of the behaviour of some aspects of the world or universe. Falsifiable hypotheses are proposed by scientists as solutions to the problem. The conjectured hypotheses are then criticized and tested. Some will be quickly eliminated. Others might prove more successful. These must be subject to even more stringent criticism and testing. When an hypothesis that has successfully withstood a wide range of rigorous tests is eventually falsified, a new problem, hopefully far removed from the original solved problem, has emerged. This new problem calls for the invention of new hypotheses, followed by renewed criticism and testing. And so the process continues indefinitely. It can never be said of a theory that it is true, however well it has withstood rigorous tests, but it can hopefully be said that a current theory is superior to its predecessors in the sense that it is able to withstand tests that falsified those predecessors.

Before we look at some examples to illustrate this falsificationist conception of the progress of science, a word should be said about the claim that "Science starts with problems". Here are some problems that have confronted scientists in the past. How are bats able to fly so dexterously at night, in spite of the fact that they have very small, weak eyes? Why is the height of a simple barometer lower at high altitudes than at low altitudes? Why were the photographic plates in Roentgen's laboratory continually becoming blackened? Why does the perihelion of the planet Mercury advance? These problems arise from more or less straightforward *observations*. In insisting on the fact that science starts with problems, then, is it not the case that, for the falsificationist just as for the naive inductivist, science starts from observation? The answer to this question is a firm "No". The observations cited above as constituting problems are only problematic *in the light of some theory*. The first is problematic in the light of the theory that living organisms "see" with their eyes; the second was problematic for the supporters of Galileo's theories because it clashed with the "force of a vacuum" theory accepted by them as an explanation of why the mercury does not fall from a barometer tube; the third was problematic for Roentgen because it was tacitly assumed at the time that no radiation or emanation of any kind existed that could penetrate the container of the photographic plates and darken them; the fourth was problematic because it was incompatible with Newton's theory. The claim that science starts with problems is perfectly compatible with the priority of theories over observation and observation statements. Science does not start with stark observation.

After this digression, we return to the falsificationist conception of the progress of science as the progression from problems to speculative hypotheses, to their criticism and eventual falsification and thence to new problems. Two examples will be offered, the first a simple one concerning the flight of bats, the second a more ambitious one concerning the progress of physics.

We start with a problem. Bats are able to fly with ease and at speed, avoiding the branches of trees, telegraph wires, other bats, etc., and can catch insects. And yet bats have weak eyes, and in any case do most of their flying at night. This poses a problem because it apparently falsifies the plausible theory that animals, like humans, see with their eyes. A falsificationist will attempt to solve the problem by making a conjecture or hypothesis. Perhaps he suggests that, although bats' eyes are apparently weak, nevertheless, in some way that is not understood, they are able to see efficiently at night by use of their eyes. This hypothesis can be tested. A sample of bats is released into a darkened room containing obstacles and their ability to avoid the obstacles measured in some way. The same bats are now blindfolded and again released into the room. Prior to the experiment, the experimenter can make the following deduction. One premise of the deduction is his hypothesis, which made quite explicit reads, "Bats are able to fly avoiding obstacles by using their eyes, and cannot do so without the use of their eyes". The second premise is a description of the experimental set-up, including the statement, "This sample of bats is blindfolded so that they do not have the use of their eyes". From these two premises, the experimenter can derive, deductively, that the sample of bats will not be able to avoid the obstacles in the test laboratory efficiently. The experiment is now performed and it is found that the bats avoid collisions just as efficiently as before. The hypothesis has been falsified. There is now a need for a fresh use of the imagination, a new conjecture or hypothesis or guess. Perhaps a scientist suggests that in some way the bat's ears are involved in its ability to avoid obstacles. The hypothesis can be tested, in an attempt to falsify it, by plugging the ears of bats before releasing them into the test laboratory. This time it is found that the ability of the bats to avoid obstacles is considerably impaired. The hypothesis has been supported. The falsificationist must now try to make his hypothesis more precise so that it becomes more readily falsifiable. It is suggested that the bat hears echoes of its own squeaks rebounding from solid objects. This is tested by gagging the bats before releasing them. Again the bats collide with obstacles and again the hypothesis is supported. The falsificationist now appears to be reaching a tentative solution to his problem, although he does not consider himself to have *proved* by experiment how bats avoid collisions while flying. Any number of factors may turn up that show him to have been mistaken. Perhaps the bat detects echoes not with its ears but with sensitive regions close to the ears, the functioning of which was impaired when the bat's ears were plugged. Or perhaps different kinds of bats detect obstacles in very different ways, so that the bats used in the experiment were not truly representative.

The progress of physics from Aristotle through Newton to Einstein provides an example on a larger scale. The falsificationist account of that progression goes something like this. Aristotelian physics was to some extent quite successful. It could explain a wide range of phenomena. It could explain why heavy objects fall to the ground (seeking their natural place at the centre of the universe), it could explain the action of siphons and liftpumps (the explanation being based on the impossibility of a vacuum), and so on. But eventually Aristotelian physics was falsified in a number of ways. Stones dropped from the top of the mast of a uniformly moving ship fell to the deck at the foot of the mast and not some distance from the mast, as Aristotle's theory predicted. The moons of Jupiter can be seen to orbit Jupiter and not the earth. A host of other falsifications were accumulated during the seventeenth century. Newton's physics, however, once it had been created and developed by way of the conjectures of the likes of Galileo and Newton, was a superior theory that superseded Aristotle's. Newton's theory could account for falling objects, the operation of siphons and liftpumps and anything else that Aristotle's theory could explain, and could also account for the phenomena that were problematic for the Aristotelians. In addition, Newton's theory could explain phenomena not touched on by Aristotle's theory, such as correlations between the tides and the location of the moon, and the variation in the force of gravity with height above the sea-bed. For two centuries, Newton's theory was successful. That is, attempts to falsify it by reference to the new phenomena predicted with its help was unsuccessful. The theory even led to the discovery of a new planet, Neptune. But in spite of its success, sustained attempts to falsify it eventually proved successful. Newton's theory was falsified in a number of ways. It was unable to account for the details of the orbit of the planet Mercury and was unable to account for the variable mass of fast-moving electrons in discharge tubes. Challenging problems faced physicists, then, as the nineteenth century gave way to the twentieth, problems calling for new speculative hypotheses designed to overcome these problems in a progressive way. Einstein was able to meet this challenge. His relativity theory was able to account for the phenomena that falsified Newton's theory, while at the same time being able to match Newton's theory in those areas where the latter had proved successful. In addition, Einstein's theory yielded the prediction of spectacular new phenomena. His special theory of relativity predicted that mass should be a function of velocity and that mass and energy could be transformed into one another, and his general theory predicted that light rays should be bent by strong gravitational fields. Attempts to refute Einstein's theory by reference to the new phenomena failed. The falsification of Einstein's theory remains as a challenge for modern physicists. Their success, if it should eventuate, would mark a new step forward in the progress of physics.

So runs a typical falsification account of the progress of physics. Later we shall have cause to doubt its accuracy and validity.

From the foregoing, it is clear that the concept of progress, of the growth of science, is a conception that is a central one in the falsificationist account of science. This issue is pursued in more detail in the next chapter.

FURTHER READING

The classic falsificationist text is Popper's *The Logic of Scientific Discovery* (London: Hutchinson, 1968). Popper's views on philosophy of science are elaborated in two collections of his papers, *Objective Knowledge* (Oxford: Oxford University Press, 1972) and *Conjectures and Refutations* (London: Routledge and Kegan Paul, 1969). A popular falsificationist essay is P. Medawar, *Induction and Intuition in Scientific Thought* (London: Methuen, 1969). Further details of reading on falsificationism are included in the reading of Chapter 5.

1. This example would be undermined if there were ways of establishing the type of inferiority complex possessed by the man in question, independently of his behaviour on the river-bank. The theory does provide scope for such a thing and the example is a totally unfair caricature.
2. K.R. Popper, *Conjectures and Refutations* (London: Routledge and Kegan Paul, 1969), p.231, italics in original.
3. J.W. Goethe, *Theory of Colours*, trans. C.L. Eastlake (Cambridge, Mass.: M.I.T. Press, 1970), p.295. See also Popper's comment on Hegel's theory of electricity in *Conjectures and Refutations*, p.332.

5

Sophisticated Falsificationism, Novel Predictions and the Growth of Science

1. Relative rather than absolute degrees of falsifiability

In the previous chapter, some conditions that an hypothesis should satisfy in order to be worthy of a scientist's consideration were mentioned. An hypothesis should be falsifiable, the more falsifiable the better, and yet should not be falsified. More sophisticated falsificationists realize that those conditions alone are insufficient. A further condition is connected with the need for science to progress. An hypothesis should be more falsifiable than the one for which it is offered as a replacement.

The sophisticated falsificationist account of science, with its emphasis on the growth of science, switches the focus of attention from the merits of a single theory to the relative merits of competing theories. It gives a dynamic picture of science rather than the static account of the most naive falsificationists. Instead of asking of a theory, "Is it falsifiable?", "How falsifiable is it?" and "Has it been falsified?", it becomes more appropriate to ask, "Is this newly proposed theory a viable replacement for the one it challenges?" In general, a newly proposed theory will be acceptable as worthy of the consideration of scientists if it is more falsifiable than its rival, and especially if it predicts a new kind of phenomenon not touched on by its rival.

The emphasis on the comparison of degrees of falsifiability of series of theories, which is a consequence of the emphasis on a science as a growing and evolving body of knowledge, enables a technical problem to be bypassed. For it is very difficult to specify just how falsifiable a single theory is. An absolute measure of falsifiability cannot be defined simply because the number of potential falsifiers of a theory will always be infinite. It is difficult to see how the question, "How falsifiable is Newton's law of gravitation?" could be answered. On the other hand, it is often possible to compare the degrees of falsifiability of laws or theories. For instance, the claim, "All pairs of bodies attract each other with a force that varies inversely as the square of their separation", is more falsifiable than the claim, "The planets in the solar system attract each other with a force that varies inversely as the square of their separation". The second is implied by the first. Anything that falsifies the second will falsify the first, but the reverse is not true. Ideally, the falsificationist would like to be able to say that the series of theories that constitute the historical evolution of a science is made up of falsifiable theories, each one in the series being more falsifiable than its predecessor.

2. Increasing falsifiability and *ad hoc* modifications

The demand that, as a science progresses, its theories should become more and more falsifiable, and consequently have more and more content and be more and more informative, rules out modifications in theories that are designed merely to protect a theory from a threatening falsification. A modification in a theory, such as the addition of an extra postulate or a change in some existing postulate, that has no testable consequences that were not already testable consequences of the unmodified theory will be called *ad hoc* modifications. The remainder of this section will consist of examples designed to clarify the notion of an *ad hoc* modification. I will first consider some *ad hoc* modifications, which the falsificationist would reject, and afterwards these will be contrasted with some modifications that are not *ad hoc* and which the falsificationist would consequently welcome.

I begin with a rather trivial example. Let us consider the generalization, "Bread nourishes". This low-level theory, if spelt out in more detail, amounts to the claim that if wheat is grown in the normal way, converted into bread in the normal way and eaten by humans in a normal way, then those humans will be nourished. This apparently innocuous theory ran into trouble in a French village on an occasion when wheat was grown in a normal way, converted into bread in a normal way and yet most people who ate the bread became seriously ill and many died. The theory, "(All) bread nourishes", was falsified. The theory can be modified to

52

avoid this falsification by adjusting it to read, "(All) bread, with the exception of that particular batch of bread produced in the French village in question, nourishes". This is an *ad hoc* modification. The modified theory cannot be tested in any way that was not also a test of the original theory. The consuming of any bread by any human constitutes a test of the original theory, whereas tests of the modified theory are restricted to the consuming of bread other than that batch of bread that led to such disastrous results in France. The modified hypothesis is less falsifiable than the original version. The falsificationist rejects such rearguard actions.

The next example is less gruesome and more entertaining. It is an example based on an interchange that actually took place in the seventeenth century between Galileo and an Aristotelian adversary. Having carefully observed the moon through his newly invented telescope, Galileo was able to report that the moon was not a smooth sphere but that its surface abounded in mountains and craters. His Aristotelian adversary had to admit that things did appear that way when he repeated the observations for himself. But the observations threatened a notion fundamental for many Aristotelians, namely, that all celestial bodies are perfect spheres. Galileo's rival defended his theory in the face of the apparent falsification in a way that was blatantly *ad hoc*. He suggested that there was an invisible substance on the moon, filling the craters and covering the mountains in such a way that the moon's shape was perfectly spherical. When Galileo inquired how the presence of the invisible substance might be detected, the reply was that there was no way in which it could be detected. There is no doubt, then, that the modified theory led to no new testable consequences and would be quite unacceptable to a falsificationist. An exasperated Galileo was able to show up the inadequacy of his rival's position in a characteristically witty way. He announced that he was prepared to admit that the invisible undetectable substance existed on the moon, but insisted that it was not disturbed in the way suggested by his rival but in fact was piled up on top of the mountains so that they were many times higher than they appeared through the telescope. Galileo was able to outmanoeuvre his rival in the fruitless game of the invention of *ad hoc* devices for the protection of theories.

One other example of a possibly *ad hoc* hypothesis from the history of science will be briefly mentioned. Prior to Lavoisier, the phlogiston theory was the standard theory of combustion. According to that theory, phlogiston is emitted from substances when they are burnt. This theory was threatened when it was discovered that many substances gain weight after combustion. One way of overcoming the apparent falsification was to suggest that phlogiston has negative weight. If this hypothesis could be tested only by weighing substances before and after combustion, then it was *ad hoc*. It led to no new tests.

Modifications of a theory in an attempt to overcome a difficulty need not be *ad hoc*. Here are some examples of modifications that are not *ad hoc,* and which consequently are acceptable from a falsificationist point of view.

Let us return to the falsification of the claim, "Bread nourishes", to see how this could be modified in an acceptable way. An acceptable move would be to replace the original falsified theory by the claim, "All bread nourishes except bread made from wheat contaminated by a particular kind of fungus" (followed by a specification of the fungus and some of its characteristics). This modified theory is not *ad hoc* because it leads to new tests. It is *independently testable,* to use Popper's phrase.[1] Possible tests would include testing the wheat from which the poisonous bread was made for the presence of the fungus, cultivating the fungus on some specially prepared wheat and testing the nourishing effect of the bread produced from it, chemically analyzing the fungus for the presence of known poisons, and so on. All these tests, many of which do not constitute tests of the original hypothesis, could result in the falsification of the modified hypothesis. If the modified, more falsifiable, hypothesis resists falsification in the face of the new tests, then something new will have been learnt and progress will have been made.

Turning now to the history of science for a less-artificial example, we might consider the train of events that led to the discovery of the planet Neptune. Nineteenth-century observations of the motion of the planet Uranus indicated that its orbit departed considerably from that predicted on the basis of Newton's gravitational theory, thus posing a problem for that theory. In an attempt to overcome the difficulty, it was suggested, by Leverrier in France and by Adams in England, that there existed a previously undetected planet in the vicinity of Uranus. The attraction between the conjectured planet and Uranus was to account for the latter's departure from its initially predicted orbit. This suggestion was not *ad hoc,* as events were to show. It was possible to estimate the approximate vicinity of the conjectural planet if it were to be of a reasonable size and to be responsible for the perturbation of

Uranus' orbit. Once this had been done, it was possible to test the new proposal by inspecting the appropriate region of the sky through a telescope. It was in this way that Galle came to make the first sighting of the planet now known as Neptune. Far from being *ad hoc,* the move to save Newton's theory from falsification by Uranus's orbit led to a new kind of test of that theory, which it was able to pass in a dramatic and progressive way.

3. Confirmation in the falsificationist account of science

When falsificationism was introduced as an alternative to inductivism in the previous chapter, falsifications, that is, the failures of theories to stand up to observational and experimental tests, were portrayed as being of key importance. It was argued that the logical situation permits the establishment of the falsity but not of the truth of theories in the light of available observation statements. It was also urged that science should progress by the proposal of bold, highly falsifiable conjectures as attempts to solve problems, followed by ruthless attempts to falsify the new proposals. Along with this came the suggestion that significant advances in science come about when those bold conjectures are falsified. The self-avowed falsificationist Popper says as much in the passage quoted on p.44, where the italics are his. However, exclusive attention to falsifying instances amounts to a misrepresentation of the more sophisticated falsificationist's position. More than a hint of this is contained in the example with which the previous section concluded. The independently testable attempt to save Newton's theory by a speculative hypothesis was a success because that hypothesis was confirmed by the discovery of Neptune and not because it was falsified.

It is a mistake to regard the falsification of bold, highly falsifiable conjectures as the occasions of significant advance in science.[2] This becomes clear when we consider the various extreme possibilities. At one extreme, we have theories that take the form of bold, risky conjectures, while at the other, we have theories that are cautious conjectures, making claims that seem to involve no significant risks. If either kind of conjecture fails an observational or experimental test it will be falsified, while if it passes such a test we will say it is *confirmed*.[3] Significant advances will be marked by the *confirmation* of *bold* conjectures or the *falsification* of *cautious* conjectures. Cases of the former kind will be informative, and constitute an important contribution to scientific knowledge, simply because they mark the discovery of something that was previously unheard of or considered unlikely. The discovery of Neptune and of radio waves and Eddington's confirmation of Einstein's risky prediction that light rays should bend in strong gravititional fields all constituted significant advances of this kind. Risky predictions were confirmed. The falsification of cautious conjectures is informative because it establishes that what was regarded as unproblematically true is in fact false. Russell's demonstration that naive set theory, which was based on what appear to be almost self-evident propositions, is inconsistent is an example of an informative falsification of a conjecture apparently free from risk. By contrast, little is learnt from the *falsification* of a *bold* conjecture or the *confirmation* óf a *cautious* conjecture. If a bold conjecture is falsified, then all that is learnt is that yet another crazy idea has been proved wrong. The falsification of Kepler's speculation that the spacing of the planetary orbits could be explained by reference to Plato's five regular solids does not mark one of the significant landmarks in the progress of physics. Similarly, the confirmation of cautious hypotheses is uninformative. Such confirmations merely indicate that some theory that was well established and regarded as unproblematic has been successfully applied once again. For instance, the confirmation of the conjecture that samples of iron extracted from its ore by some new process will, like other iron, expand when heated, would be of little consequence.

The falsificationist wishes to reject *ad hoc* hypotheses and to encourage the proposal of bold hypotheses as potential improvements on falsified theories. Those bold hypotheses will lead to novel, testable predictions, which do not follow from the original, falsified theory. However, while the fact that it does lead to the possibility of new tests makes an hypothesis worthy of investigation, it will not rank as an improvement on the problematic theory it is designed to replace until it has survived at least some of those tests. This is tantamount to saying that before it can be regarded as an adequate replacement for a falsified theory, a newly and boldly proposed theory must make some novel predictions that are confirmed. Many wild and rash speculations will not survive subsequent testing and consequently will not be rated as contributing to the growth of scientific knowledge. The occasional wild and rash speculation that does lead to a novel, unlikely prediction, which is nevertheless confirmed by observation or experiment, will thereby become established as a highlight in the history of the growth of science. The *confirmations* of novel predictions resulting from bold conjectures are very important in the falsificationist account of the growth of science.

4. Boldness, novelty and background knowledge

A little more needs to be said about the adjectives "bold" and "novel" as applied to hypotheses and predictions respectively. They are both historically relative notions. What rates as a bold conjecture at one stage in the history of science need no longer be bold at some later stage. When Maxwell proposed his "dynamical theory of the electromagnetic field" in 1864, it was a bold conjecture. It was bold because it conflicted with theories generally accepted at the time, theories that included the assumption that electromagnetic systems (magnets, charged bodies, current-carrying conductors, etc.) act upon each other instantaneously across empty space and that electromagnetic effects can be propagated at a finite velocity only through material substances. Maxwell's theory clashed with these generally accepted assumptions because it predicted that light is an electromagnetic phenomenon and also predicted, as was to be realized later, that fluctuating currents should emit a new kind of radiation, radio waves, travelling at a finite velocity through empty space. In 1864, therefore, Maxwell's theory was bold and the subsequent prediction of radio waves was a *novel* prediction. Today, the fact that Maxwell's theory can give an accurate account of the behaviour of a wide range of electromagnetic systems is a generally accepted part of scientific knowledge, and assertions about the existence and properties of radio waves will not rate as novel predictions.

If we call the complex of scientific theories generally accepted and well established at some stage in the history of science the *background knowledge* of the time, then we can say that a conjecture will be bold if its claims are unlikely in the light of the background knowledge of the time. Einstein's general theory of relativity was a bold one in 1915 because at that time background knowledge included the assumption that light travels in straight lines. This clashed with one consequence of general relativity, namely, that light rays should bend in strong gravitational fields. Copernicus's astronomy was bold in 1543 because it clashed with the background assumption that the earth is stationery at the centre of the universe. It would not be considered bold today.

Just as conjectures will be considered bold or otherwise by reference to the relevant background knowledge, so predictions will be judged novel if they involve some phenomenon that does not figure in, or is perhaps explicitly ruled out by, the background knowledge of the time. The prediction of Neptune in 1846 was a novel one because the background knowledge at that time contained no reference to such a planet. The prediction that Poisson deduced from Fresnel's wave theory of light in 1818, namely, that a bright spot should be observed at the centre of one side of an opaque disc suitably illuminated from the other, was novel because the existence of that bright spot was ruled out by the particle theory of light that formed part of the background knowledge of the time.

In the previous section, it was argued that major contributions to the growth of scientific knowledge come about either when a bold conjecture is confirmed or when a cautious conjecture is falsified. The idea of background knowledge enables us to see that these two possibilities will occur together as the result of a single experiment. Background knowledge consists of cautious hypotheses just because that knowledge is well established and considered to be unproblematic. The confirmation of a bold conjecture will involve the falsification of some part of the background knowledge with respect to which the conjecture was bold.

5. Comparison of the inductivist and falsificationist view of confirmation

We have seen that confirmation has an important role to play in science as interpreted by the sophisticated falsificationist. However, this does not invalidate the labelling of that position "falsificationism". It is still maintained by the sophisticated falsificationist that theories can be falsified and rejected while it is denied that theories can ever be established as true or probably true. The aim of science is to falsify theories and to replace them by better theories, theories that demonstrate a greater ability to withstand tests. Confirmations of new theories are important insofar as they constitute evidence that a new theory is an improvement on the theory it replaces, the theory that is falsified by the evidence unearthed with the aid of, and confirming, the new theory. Once a newly proposed bold theory has succeeded in ousting its rival, then it in turn becomes a new target at which stringent tests should be directed, tests devised with the aid of further boldly conjectured theories.

What is this thing called Science?

Because of the falsificationists' emphasis on the growth of science, their account of confirmation is significantly different from that of the inductivists. The significance of some confirming instances of a theory according to the inductivist position described in Chapter 1 is determined solely by the logical relationship between the observation statements that are confirmed and the theory that they support. The degree of support given to Newton's theory by Galle's observation of Neptune is no different from the degree of support given by a modern observation of Neptune. The historical context in which the evidence is acquired is irrelevant. Confirming instances are such if they give inductive support to a theory, and the greater the number of confirming instances established, the greater the support for the theory and the more likely it is to be true. This ahistorical theory of confirmation would seem to have the unappealing consequence that innumerable observations made on falling stones, planetary positions, etc. will constitute worthwhile scientific activity insofar as they will lead to increases in the estimate of the probability of the truth of the law of gravitation.

By contrast, in the falsificationist account, the significance of confirmations depends very much on their historical context. A confirmation will confer some high degree of merit on a theory if that confirmation resulted from the testing of a novel prediction. That is, a confirmation will be significant if it is estimated that it is unlikely to eventuate in the light of the background knowledge of the time. Confirmations that are foregone conclusions are insignificant. If today I confirm Newton's theory by dropping a stone to the ground, I contribute nothing of value to science. On the other hand, if tomorrow I confirm a speculative theory implying that the gravitational attraction between two bodies depends on their temperature, falsifying Newton's theory in the process, I would have made a significant contribution to scientific knowledge. Newton's theory of gravitation and some of its limitations are part of current background knowledge, whereas a temperature dependence of gravitational attraction is not. Here is one further example in support of the historical perspective that the falsificationists introduce into confirmation. Hertz confirmed Maxwell's theory when he detected the first radio waves. I also confirm Maxwell's theory whenever I listen to my radio. The logical situation is similar in the two cases. In each case, the theory predicts that radio waves should be detected and, in each case, their successful detection lends some inductive support to the theory. Nevertheless,

Hertz is justly famous for the confirmation he achieved, whereas my frequent confirmations are rightly ignored in a scientific context. Hertz made a significant step forward. When I listen to my radio I am only marking time. The historical context makes all the difference.

FURTHER READING

Popper's writings have already been referred to as reading relevant to falsificationism. Especially relevant to discussions of the growth of science is *Conjectures and Refutations* (London: Routledge and Kegan Paul, 1969), Ch. 10 and *Objective Knowledge* (Oxford: Oxford University Press, 1972), Ch. 5 and 7. Feyerabend has made contributions to the more sophisticated falsificationist programme. See, for instance, his "Explanation, Reduction and Empiricism", in *Scientific Explanation, Space and Time, Minnesota Studies in the Philosophy of Science,* vol.3, ed. H. Feigl and G. Maxwell (Minneapolis: University of Minnesota Press, 1962), pp.27-97, and "Problems of Empiricism", in *Beyond the Edge of Certainty,* ed. R. Colodny (New York: Prentice-Hall, 1965), pp.45-260. I. Lakatos discusses various stages in the development of the falsificationist programme and its relation to the inductivist programme in "Falsification and the Methodology of Scientific Research Programmes", in *Criticism and the Growth of Knowledge,* ed. I. Lakatos and A. Musgrave (Cambridge: Cambridge University Press, 1974), pp.91-196, and he applies the falsificationist concept of growth to mathematics in "Proofs and Refutations", *British Journal for the Philosophy of Science* 14 (1963-64): 1-25, 120-39, 221-342. Interesting discussions of the growth of science are Noretta Koertge, "Theory Change in Science", in *Conceptual Change,* ed. G. Pearce and P. Maynard (Dordrecht: Reidel Publ. Co., 1973), pp.167-98; S. Amsterdamski, *Between Science and Metaphysics* (Dordrecht: Reidel Publ. Co., 1975); and H.R. Post, "Correspondence, Invariance and Heuristics", *Studies in History and Philosophy of Science* 2 (1971): 213-55.

1. See, for example, K.R. Popper, "The Aim of Science", in his *Objective Knowledge* (Oxford: Oxford University Press, 1972), pp.191-205, especially p.193.
2. For a detailed discussion of this point, see A.F. Chalmers, "On Learning from Our Mistakes", *British Journal for the Philosophy of Science* 24 (1973): 164-173.
3. This usage of "confirmed" should not be confused with another usage, according to which to say of a theory that it is confirmed is to claim that it has been proved or established as true.

6

The Limitations of Falsificationism

1. Theory-dependence of observation and the fallibility of falsifications

The naive falsificationist insists that scientific activity should be concerned with attempts to falsify theories by establishing the truth of observation statements that are inconsistent with them. The more sophisticated falsificationist realizes the inadequacy of this and recognizes the importance of the role played by confirmation of speculative theories as well as the falsification of well-established ones. One thing that both types of falsificationist hold in common, however, is that there is an important qualitative difference in the status of confirmations and falsifications. Theories can be conclusively falsified in the light of suitable evidence, whereas they can never be established as true or even probably true whatever the evidence. Theory acceptance is always tentative. Theory rejection can be decisive. This is the factor that earns falsificationists their title.

The claims of the falsificationist are seriously undermined by the fact that observation statements are theory-dependent and fallible. This can be seen immediately when one recalls the logical point invoked by the falsificationists in support of their case. If true observation statements are given, *then* it is possible to logically deduce from them the falsity of some universal statements, whereas it is not possible to deduce from them the truth of any universal statements. This is an unexceptional point, but it is a conditional one based on the assumption that perfectly secure observation statements are available. But they are not, as was argued at length in Chapter 3. All observation statements are fallible. Consequently, if a universal statement or complex of universal statements constituting a theory or part of a theory clashes with some observation statement, it may be the observation statement that is at fault. Nothing in the logic of the situation requires that it should always be the theory that is rejected on the occasion of a clash with observation. A fallible observation statement might be rejected and the fallible theory with which it clashes retained. This is precisely what was involved when Copernicus's theory was retained and the naked-eye observation that Venus does not change size appreciably during the course of the year, which is inconsistent with the Copernican theory, was rejected. It is also what is involved when modern descriptions of the moon's trajectory are retained and observation statements referring to the fact that the moon is much larger when it is near the horizon than when it is high in the sky are regarded as resulting from an illusion, even though the cause of the illusion is not well understood. Science abounds with examples of the rejection of observation statements and the retention of the theories with which they clash. However securely based on observation a statement may seem to be, the possibility that new theoretical advances will reveal inadequacies in that statement cannot be ruled out. Consequently, straightforward, conclusive falsifications of theories are not achievable.

2. Popper's inadequate defence

Popper was aware of the problem discussed in section 1 right from the time he first published the German version of his book *The Logic of Scientific Discovery* in 1934. In Chapter 5 of that book, entitled "The Problem of the Empirical Base", he set out an account of observation and observation statements that took account of the fact that infallible observation statements are not given directly through sensory preceptions. In this section, I will first summarize his account, and then argue that it does not save the falsificationist from the objections of section 1.

Popper's position highlights the important distinction between public observation statements on the one hand and the private perceptual experiences of individual observers on the other. The latter are in some sense "given" to individuals in the act of observing, but there is no straightforward step from those private experiences (which will depend on factors peculiar to each individual observer such as his expectations, prior knowledge, etc.) to an observation statement that is meant to describe the observed situation. An observation statement, formulated in a public language, will be testable and open to modification or rejection. Individual observers may or may not accept a particular observation statement. Their *decision* on the matter will be *motivated* in part by the relevant perceptual experiences, but no perceptual experience on the part of an individual will be sufficient to establish the validity of an observation statement. An observer may be led to accept some observation statement on the basis of a perception and yet that observation statement may be false.

These points can be illustrated by the following examples. "Moons of Jupiter are visible through a telescope" and "Mars is square and intensely coloured" are public observation statements. The first might well have been uttered by Galileo or a supporter and the second was recorded in Kepler's notebook. Both are public, in the sense that they can be entertained and criticized by anyone who has the opportunity to do so. The Galileans' decision to defend the first was motivated by the perceptual experiences that accompanied their telescopic sightings of Jupiter, and Kepler's decision to record the second was likewise based on his perceptual experiences when directing a telescope towards Mars. Both observation statements are testable. Galileo's adversaries insisted that the patches that Galileo had interpreted as moons of Jupiter were aberrations attributable to the functioning of the telescope. Galileo defended his claim about the visibility of Jupiter's moons by arguing that if the moons were aberrations, then moons should appear near the other planets also. The public debate continued, and in this particular case, as telescopes were improved and optical theory developed, the observation statement referring to the moons of Jupiter survived the criticism levelled at it. Most scientists eventually decided to accept the statement. By contrast, Kepler's statement concerning the shape and colour of Mars did not survive criticism and tests. It was soon decided to reject the statement.

The essence of Popper's position on observation statements is that their acceptability is gauged by their ability to survive tests. Those that fail subsequent tests are rejected, while those that survive all the tests to which they are subjected are tentatively retained. In his early work at least, Popper emphasizes the role of decisions made on the part of individuals and groups of individuals to accept or reject what I have called observation statements, and what Popper refers to as "basic statements". Thus he writes, "Basic statements are accepted as the result of a decision or agreement, and to that extent they are conventions",[1] and again,

Any empirical scientific statement can be presented (by describing experimental arrangements etc.) in such a way that anyone who has learned the relevant technique can test it. If, as a result, he rejects the statement, then it will not satisfy us if he tells us all about his feelings of doubt or about his feelings of conviction as to his perceptions. What he must do is to formulate an assertion which contradicts our own, and give us his instruction for testing it. If he fails to do this, we can only ask him to take another and perhaps a more careful look at our experiment, and think again.[2]

Popper's emphasis on the conscious decisions of individuals introduces a subjective element that clashes somewhat with Popper's later insistence on science as "a process without a subject". This matter will be discussed more fully in later chapters. For the present, I would prefer to reformulate Popper's position on observation statements in a less subjective way, thus: An observation statement is acceptable, tentatively, at a particular stage in the development of a science, if it is able to withstand all the tests made possible by the state of development of the science in question at that stage.

According to the Popperian position, the observation statements that form the basis with respect to which the merit of a scientific theory is to be assessed are themselves fallible. Popper emphasizes the point with a striking metaphor.

The empirical basis of objective science has thus nothing "absolute" about it. Science does not rest upon solid bedrock. The bold structure of its theories rises, as it were above a swamp. It is like a building erected on piles. The piles are driven down from above into the swamp, but not down to any natural or "given" base; and if we stop driving the piles deeper, it is not because we have reached firm ground. We simply stop when we are satisfied that the piles are firm enough to carry the structure, as least for the time being.[3]

But it is precisely the fact that observation statements are fallible, and their acceptance only tentative and open to revision, that undermines the falsificationist position. Theories cannot be conclusively falsified because the observation statements that form the basis for the falsification may themselves prove to be false in the light of later developments. Knowledge available at the time of Copernicus did not permit a legitimate criticism of the observation that the apparent sizes of Mars and Venus remain roughly constant, so that Copernicus's theory, taken literally, could be deemed falsified by that observation. One hundred years later, the falsification could be revoked because of new developments in optics.

Conclusive falsifications are ruled out by the lack of a perfectly secure observational base on which they depend.

3. The complexity of realistic test situations

"All swans are white" is certainly falsified if an instance of a non-white swan can be established. But simplified illustrations of the logic of a falsification such as this disguise a serious difficulty for falsificationism that arises from the complexity of any realistic test situation. A realistic scientific theory will consist of a complex of universal statements rather than a single statement like "All swans are white". Further, if a theory is to be experimentally tested, then more will be involved than those statements that constitute the theory under test. The theory will need to be augmented by auxiliary assumptions, such as laws and theories governing the use of any instruments used, for instance. In addition, in order to deduce some prediction the validity of which is to be experimentally tested it will be necessary to add initial conditions such as a decription of the experimental set-up. For instance, suppose an astronomical theory is to be tested by observing the position of some planet through a telescope. The theory must predict the orientation of the telescope necessary for a sighting of the planet at some specified time. The premises from which the prediction is derived will include the interconnected statements that constitute the theory under test, initial conditions such as previous positions of the planet and sun, auxiliary assumptions such as those enabling corrections to be made for refraction of light from the planet in the earth's atmosphere, and so on. Now if the prediction that follows from this maze of premises turns out to be false (in our example, if the planet does not appear at the predicted location), then all that the logic of the situation permits us to conclude is that at least one of the premises must be false. It does not enable us to identify the faulty premise. It may be the theory under test that is at fault, but alternatively it may be an auxiliary assumption or some part of the description of the initial conditions that is responsible for the incorrect prediction. A theory cannot be conclusively falsified, because the possibility that some part of the complex test situation, other than the theory under test, is responsible for an erroneous prediction cannot be ruled out.

Here are some examples from the history of astronomy that illustrate the point.

In an example utilized previously, we discussed how Newton's theory was apparently refuted by the orbit of the planet Uranus. In this case, it turned out not to be the theory at fault but the description of the initial conditions, which did not include a consideration of the yet-to-be-discovered planet Neptune. A second example involves an argument by means of which the Danish astronomer Tycho Brahé claimed to have refuted the Copernician theory a few decades after the first publication of that theory. If the earth orbits the sun, Brahé argued, then the direction in which a fixed star is observed from earth should vary during the course of the year as the earth moves from one side of the sun to the other. But when Brahé tried to detect this predicted parallax with his instruments, which were the most accurate and sensitive ones in existence at the time, he failed. This led Brahé to conclude that the Copernican theory was false. With hindsight, it can be appreciated that it was not the Copernican theory that was responsible for the faulty prediction, but one of Brahé's auxiliary assumptions. Brahé's estimate of the distance of the fixed stars was many times too small. When his estimate is replaced by a more realistic one, the predicted parallax turns out to be too small to be detectable by Brahé's instruments.

A third example is a hypothetical one devised by Imre Lakatos. It reads as follows:

> The story is about an imaginary case of planetary misbehaviour. A physicist of the pre Einsteinian era takes Newton's mechanics and his law of gravitation, N, the accepted initial conditions, I, and calculates, with their help, the path of a newly discovered small planet, p. But the planet deviates from the calculated path. Does our Newtonian physicist consider that the deviation was forbidden by Newton's theory and therefore that, once established, it refutes the theory N? No. He suggests that there must be a hitherto unknown planet p', which perturbs the path of p. He calculates the mass, orbit, etc. of this hypothetical planet and then asks an experimental astronomer to test his hypothesis. The planet p' is so small that even the biggest available telescopes cannot possibly observe it; the experimental astronomer applies for a research grant to build yet a bigger one. In three years time, the new telescope is ready. Were the unknown planet p' to be discovered, it would be hailed as a new victory of Newtonian science. But it is not. Does our scientist abandon Newton's theory and his idea of the perturbing planet? No. He suggests that a cloud of cosmic dust hides the planet from us. He calculates the location and properties of this cloud and asks for a research grant to send up a satellite to test his calculations. Were the satellite's instruments (possibly new ones, based on a little-tested theory)

to record the existence of the conjectural cloud, the result would be hailed as an outstanding victory for Newtonian science. But the cloud is not found. Does our scientist abandon Newton's theory, together with the idea of the perturbing planet and the idea of the cloud which hides it? No. He suggests that there is some magnetic field in that region of the universe which disturbed the instruments of the satellite. A new satellite is sent up. Were the magnetic field to be found, Newtonians would celebrate a sensational victory. But it is not. Is this regarded as a refutation of Newtonian science? No. Either yet another ingenious auxiliary hypothesis is proposed or . . . the whole story is buried in the dusty volumes of periodicals and the story never mentioned again.[4]

If this story is regarded as a plausible one, it illustrates how a theory can always be protected from falsification by deflecting the falsification to some other part of the complex web of assumptions.

4. Falsificationism inadequate on historical grounds

An embarrassing historical fact for falsificationists is that if their methodology had been strictly adhered to by scientists then those theories generally regarded as being among the best examples of scientific theories would never have been developed because they would have been rejected in their infancy. Given any example of a classic scientific theory, whether at the time of its first proposal or at a later date, it is possible to find observational claims that were generally accepted at the time and were considered to be inconsistent with the theory. Nevertheless, those theories were not rejected, and it is fortunate for science that they were not. Some historical examples to support my claim follow.

In the early years of its life, Newton's gravitional theory was falsified by observations of the moon's orbit. It took almost fifty years to deflect this falsification on to causes other than Newton's theory. Later in its life, the same theory was known to be inconsistent with the details of the orbit of the planet Mercury, although scientists did not abandon the theory for that reason. It turned out that it was never possible to explain away this falsification in a way that protected Newton's theory.

A second example concerns Bohr's theory of the atom, and is due to Lakatos.[5] Early versions of the theory were inconsistent with the observation that some matter is stable for a time that exceeds about 10^{-8} seconds. According to the theory, negatively charged electrons within atoms orbit around positively charged nuclei. But according to the classical electromagnetic theory presupposed by Bohr's theory, orbiting electrons should radiate. The radiation would result in an orbiting electron losing energy and collapsing into the nucleus. The quantitative details of classical electromagnetism yield an estimated time of about 10^{-8} seconds for this collapse to occur. Fortunately, Bohr presevered with his theory, in spite of this falsification.

A third example concerns the kinetic theory and has the advantage that the falsification of that theory at birth was explicitly acknowledged by its originator. When Maxwell published the first details of the kinetic theory of gases in 1859, in that very same paper he acknowledged the fact that the theory was falsified by measurements on the specific heats of gases.[6] Eighteen years later, commenting on the consequences of the kinetic theory, he wrote.

> Some of these, no doubt, are very satisfactory to us in our present state of opinion about the constitution of bodies, but there are others which are likely to startle us out of our complacency and perhaps ultimately to drive us out of all the hypotheses in which we have hitherto found refuge into that thoroughly conscious ignorance which is a prelude to every real advance in knowledge.[7]

All the important developments within the kinetic theory took place after this falsification. Once again, it is fortunate that the theory was not abandoned in the face of falsifications by measurements of the specific heats of gases, as the naive falsificationist at least would be forced to insist.

A fourth example, the Copernican Revolution, will be outlined in more detail in the following section. This example will emphasize the difficulties that arise for the falsificationist when the complexities of major theory changes are taken into account. The example will also set the scene for a discussion of some more recent and more adequate attempts to characterize the essence of science and its methods.

5. The Copernican Revolution

It was generally accepted in mediaeval Europe that the earth lies at the centre of a finite universe and that the sun, planets and stars orbit around it. The physics and cosmology that provided the framework in which this astronomy was set was basically that developed by Aristotle in the fourth century B.C. In the second

What is this thing called Science?

century A.D., Ptolemy devised a detailed astronomical system that specified the orbits of the moon, the sun and all the planets.

In the early decades of the sixteenth century, Copernicus devised a new astronomy, an astronomy involving a moving earth, which challenged the Aristotelian and Ptolemaic system. According to the Copernican view, the earth is not stationary at the centre of the universe but orbits the sun along with the planets. By the time Copernicus's idea had been substantiated, the Aristotelian world view had been replaced by the Newtonian one. The details of the story of this major theory change, a change that took place over one and a half centuries, do not lend support to the methodologies advocated by the inductivists and falsificationists, and indicate a need for a different, more complexly structured account of science and its growth.

When Copernicus first published the details of his new astronomy, in 1543, there were many arguments that could be, and were, levelled against it. Relative to the scientific knowledge of the time, these arguments were sound ones and Copernicus could not satisfactorily defend his theory against them. In order to appreciate this situation, it is necessary to be familiar with some aspects of the Aristotelian world view on which the arguments against Copernicus were based. A very brief sketch of some of the relevant points follows.

The Aristotelian universe was divided into two distinct regions. The sub-lunar region was the inner region, extending from the central earth to just inside the moon's orbit. The super-lunar region was the remainder of the finite universe, extending from the moon's orbit to the sphere of the stars, which marked the outer boundary of the universe. Nothing existed beyond the outer sphere, not even space. Unfilled space is an impossibility in the Aristotelian system. All celestial objects in the super-lunar region were made of an incorruptible element called aether. Aether possessed a natural propensity to move around the centre of the universe in perfect circles. This basic idea became modified and extended in Ptolemy's astronomy. Since observations of planetary positions at various times could not be reconciled with circular, earth-centred orbits, Ptolemy introduced further circles, called epicycles, into the system. Planets moved in circles, or epicycles, the centres of which moved in circles around the earth. The orbits could be further refined by adding epicycles to epicycles etc. in such a way that the resulting system was compatible with observations of planetary positions and capable of predicting future planetary positions.

In contrast to the orderly, regular, incorruptible character of the super-lunar region, the sub-lunar region was marked by change, growth and decay, generation and corruption. All substances in the sub-lunar region were mixtures of four elements, air, earth, fire and water, and the relative proportions of elements in a mixture determined the properties of the substance so constituted. Each element had a natural place in the universe. The natural place for earth was at the centre of the universe; for water, on the surface of the earth; for air, in the region immediately above the surface of the earth; and for fire, at the top of the atmosphere, close to the moon's orbit. Consequently, each earthly object would have a natural place in the sub-lunar region depending on the relative proportion of the four elements that it contained. Stones, being mostly earth, have a natural place near the centre of the earth, while flames, being mostly fire, have a natural place near to the moon's orbit, and so on. All objects have a propensity to move in straight lines, upwards or downwards, towards their natural place. Thus stones have a natural motion straight downwards, towards the centre of the earth, and flames have a natural motion straight upwards, away from the centre of the earth. All motions other than natural motions require a cause. For instance, arrows need to be propelled by a bow and chariots need to be drawn by horses.

These, then, are the bare bones of the Aristotelian mechanics and cosmology that were presupposed by contemporaries of Copernicus, and which were utilized in arguments against a moving earth. Let us look at some of the forceful arguments against the Copernican system.

Perhaps the argument that constituted the most serious threat to Copernicus was the so-called tower argument. It runs as follows. If the earth spins on its axis, as Copernicus had it, then any point on the earth's surface will move a considerable distance in a second. If a stone is dropped from the top of a tower erected on the moving earth, it will execute its natural motion and fall towards the centre of the earth. While it is doing so the tower will be sharing the motion of the earth, due to its spinning. Consequently, by the time the stone reaches the surface of the earth the tower will have moved around from the position it occupied at the beginning of the stone's downward journey. The stone should therefore strike the ground some distance from the foot of the tower. But this does not happen in practice. The stones strikes the ground at the base of the tower. It follows that the earth cannot be spinning and that Copernicus's theory is false.

What is this thing called Science?

Another mechanical argument against Copernicus concerns loose objects such as stones, philosophers, etc. resting on the surface of the earth. If the earth spins, why are such objects not flung from the earth's surface, as stones would be flung from the rim of a rotating wheel? And if the earth, as well as spinning, moves bodily around the sun, why doesn't it leave the moon behind?

Some arguments against Copernicus based on astronomical considerations have been mentioned earlier in this book. They involved the absence of parallax in the observed positions of the stars and the fact that Mars and Venus, as viewed by the naked eye, do not change size appreciably during the course of the year.

Because of the arguments I have mentioned, and others like them, the supporters of the Copernican theory were faced with serious difficulties. Copernicus himself was very much immersed in Aristotelian metaphysics and had no adequate response to them.

In view of the strength of the case against Copernicus, it might well be asked just what there was to be said in favour of the Copernican theory in 1543. The answer is, "not very much". The main attraction of the Copernican theory lay in the neat way it explained a number of features of planetary motion, which could be explained in the rival Ptolemaic theory only in an unattractive, artificial way. The features are the retrograde motion of the planets and the fact that, unlike the other planets, Mercury and Venus always remain in the proximity of the sun. A planet at regular intervals regresses, that is, stops its westward motion among the stars (as viewed from earth) and for a short time retraces its path eastward before continuing its journey westward once again. In the Ptolemaic system, retrograde motion was explained by the somewhat *ad hoc* manoeuvre of adding epicycles especially designed for the purpose. In the Copernican system, no such artificial move is necessary. Retrograde motion is a natural consequence of the fact that the earth and the planets together orbit the sun against the background of the fixed stars. Similar remarks apply to the problem of the constant proximity of the sun, Mercury and Venus. This is a natural consequence of the Copernican system once it is established that the orbits of Mercury and Venus are inside that of the earth. In the Ptolemaic system, the orbits of the sun, Mercury and Venus have to be artificially linked together to achieve the required result.

There were some mathematical features of the Copernican theory that were in its favour, then. Apart from these, the two rival systems were more or less on a par as far as simplicity and accord with observations of planetary positions are concerned. Circular sun-centred orbits cannot be reconciled with observation, so that Copernicus, like Ptolemy, needed to add epicycles, and the total number of epicycles needed to produce orbits in accord with known observations was about the same for the two systems. In 1543, the arguments from mathematical simplicity that worked in favour of Copernicus could not be regarded as an adequate counter to the mechanical and astronomical arguments that worked against him. Nevertheless, a number of mathematically capable natural philosophers were to be attracted to the Copernican system, and their efforts to defend it became increasingly successful over the next hundred years or so.

The person who contributed most significantly to the defence of the Copernican system was Galileo. He did so in two ways. Firstly, he used a telescope to observe the heavens, and in so doing he transformed the observational data that the Copernican theory was required to explain.[8] Secondly, he devised the beginnings of a new mechanics that was to replace Aristotelian mechanics and with reference to which the mechanical arguments against Copernicus were defused.

When, in 1609, Galileo constructed his first telescopes and trained them on the heavens, he made dramatic discoveries. He saw that there were many stars invisible to the naked eye. He saw that Jupiter had moons and he saw that the surface of the earth's moon was covered with mountains and craters. He also observed that the apparent size of Mars and Venus, as viewed through the telescope, changed in the way predicted by the Copernican system. Later, Galileo was to confirm that Venus had phases like the moon, as Copernicus had predicted but which clashed with Ptolemy's system. The moons of Jupiter defused the Aristotelian argument against Copernicus based on the fact that the moon stays with an allegedly moving earth. For now Aristotelians were faced with the same problem with respect to Jupiter and its moons. The earthlike surface of the moon undermined the Aristotelian distinction between the perfect, incorruptible heavens and the changing, corruptible earth. The discovery of the phases of Venus marked a success for the Copernicans and a new problem for the Ptolemaics. It is undeniable that once the observations made by Galileo through his telescope are accepted, the difficulties facing the Copernican theory are diminished.

The foregoing remarks on Galileo and the telescope raise a serious epistemological problem. Why should observations through a telescope be preferred to naked-eye observations? One answer to this question might utilize an optical theory of the telescope that explains its magnifying properties and that also gives an account of the various aberrations to which we can expect telescopic images to be subject. But Galileo himself did not utilize an optical theory for that purpose. The first optical theory capable of giving support in this direction was devised by Galileo's contemporary, Kepler, early in the sixteenth century, and this theory was improved and augmented in later decades. A second way of facing our question concerning the superiority of telescopic to naked-eye observations is to demonstrate the effectiveness of the telescope in a practical way, by focusing it on distant towers, ships, etc. and demonstrating how the instrument magnifies and renders objects more distinctly visible. However, there is a difficulty with this kind of justification of the use of the telescope in astronomy. When terrestrial objects are viewed through a telescope, it is possible to separate the viewed object from aberrations contributed by the telescope because of the observer's familiarity with what a tower, a ship, etc. looks like. This does not apply when an observer searches the heavens for he knows not what. It is significant in this respect that Galileo's drawing of the moon's surface as he saw it through a telescope contains some craters that do not in fact exist there. Presumably those "craters" were aberrations arising from the functioning of Galileo's far-from-perfect telescopes. Enough has been said in this paragraph to indicate that the justification of telescopic observations was no simple, straightfoward matter. Those adversaries of Galileo who queried his findings were not all stupid, stubborn reactionaries. Justifications were forthcoming, and became more and more adequate as better and better telescopes were constructed and as optical theories of their functioning were developed. But all this took time.

Galileo's greatest contribution to science was his work in mechanics. He laid some of the foundations of the Newtonian mechanics that was to replace Aristotle's. He distinguished clearly between velocity and acceleration and asserted that freely falling objects move with a constant acceleration that is independent of their weight, dropping a distance proportional to the square of the time of fall. He denied the Aristotelian claim that all motion requires a cause and in its place proposed a circular law of inertia, according to which a moving object subject to no forces will move indefinitely in a circle around the earth at uniform speed. He analyzed projectile motion by resolving the motion of a projectile into a horizontal component moving with a constant velocity obeying his law of inertia, and a vertical component subject to a constant acceleration downwards. He showed that the resulting path of a projectile was a parabola. He developed the concept of relative motion and argued that the uniform motion of a system could not be detected by mechanical means without access to some reference point outside of the system.

These major developments were not achieved instantaneously by Galileo. They emerged gradually over a period of half a century, culminating in his book *Two New Sciences,*[9] which was first published in 1638, almost a century after the publication of Copernicus's major work. Galileo rendered his new conceptions meaningful and increasingly more precise by means of illustrations and thought experiments. Occasionally, Galileo described actual experiments, for instance, experiments involving the rolling of spheres down inclined planes, although just how many of these Galileo actually performed is a matter of some dispute.

Galileo's new mechanics enabled the Copernican system to be defended against some of the objections to it mentioned above. An object held at the top of a tower and sharing with the tower a circular motion around the earth's centre will continue in that motion, along with the tower, after it is dropped and will consequently strike the ground at the foot of the tower, consistent with experience. Galileo took the argument further and claimed that the correctness of his law of inertia could be demonstrated by dropping a stone from the top of the mast of a uniformly moving ship and noting that it strikes the deck at the foot of the mast, although Galileo did not claim to have performed the experiment. Galileo was less successful in explaining why loose objects are not flung from the surface of a spinning earth. With hindsight, this can be attributed to the inadequacies of his principle of inertia and of his lack of a clear conception of gravity as a force.

Although the bulk of Galileo's scientific work was designed to strengthen the Copernican theory, Galileo did not himself devise a detailed astronomy, and seemed to follow the Aristotelians in their preference for circular orbits. It was Galileo's contemporary, Kepler, who contributed a major breakthrough in that direction when he discovered that each planetary orbit could be represented by a single ellipse, with the sun at one focus. This eliminated the complex system of epicycles that both Copernicus and Ptolemy had found necessary. No similar simplification is possible in the Ptolemaic, earth-centre system. Kepler had at his disposal Tycho Brahe's recordings of planetary positions, which were more accurate than those available to Copernicus. After a painstaking analysis of the data, Kepler arrived at his three laws of planetary motion, that planets move in elliptical orbits around the sun, that a line joining a planet to the sun sweeps out equal areas in equal times, and that the square of the period of a planet is proportional to the cube of its mean distance from the sun.

Galileo and Kepler certainly strengthened the case in favour of the Copernican theory. However, more developments were necessary before that theory was securely based on a comprehensive physics. Newton was able to take advantage of the work of Galileo, Kepler and others to construct that comprehensive physics that he published in his *Principia* in 1687. He spelt out a clear conception of force as the cause of acceleration rather than motion, a conception that had been present in a somewhat confused way in the writings of Galileo and Kepler. Newton replaced Galileo's law of circular inertia with his own law of linear inertia, according to which bodies continue to move in straight lines at uniform speed unless acted on by a force. Another major contribution by Newton was of course his law of gravitation. This enabled Newton to explain the approximate correctness of Kepler's laws of planetary motion and Galileo's law of free fall. In the Newtonian system, the realms of the celestial bodies and of earthly bodies were unified, each set of bodies moving under the influence of forces according to Newton's laws of motion. Once Newton's physics had been constituted, it was possible to apply it in detail to astronomy. It was possible, for instance, to investigate the details of the moon's orbit, taking into account its finite size, the spin of the earth, the wobble of the earth upon its axis, and so on. It was also possible to investigate the departure of the planets from Kepler's laws due to the finite mass of the sun, interplanetary forces, etc. Developments such as these were to occupy some of Newton's successors for the next couple of centuries.

The story I have sketched here should be sufficient to indicate that the Copernican Revolution did not take place at the drop of a hat or two from the Leaning Tower of Pisa. It is also clear that neither the inductivists nor the falsificationists give an account of science that is compatible with it. New concepts of force and inertia did not come about as a result of careful observation and experiment. Nor did they come about through the falsification of bold conjectures and the continual replacement of one bold conjecture by another. Early formulations of the new theory, involving imperfectly formulated novel conceptions, were persevered with and developed in spite of apparent falsifications. It was only after a new system of physics had been devised, a process that involved the intellectual labour of many scientists over several centuries, that the new theory could be successfully matched with the results of observation and experiment in a detailed way. No account of science can be regarded as anywhere near adequate unless it can accommodate such factors.

FURTHER READING

Lakatos's criticism of anything but the most sophisticated brands of falsificationism is in his article "Falsification and the Methodology of Scientific Research Programmes", in *Criticism and the Growth of Knowledge,* ed. I. Lakatos and A. Musgrave (Cambridge: Cambridge University Press, 1974), pp.91-196. Other classic criticisms are in P. Duhem, *The Aim and Structure of Physical Theory* (New York: Athenum, 1962) and W.V.O. Quine's article "Two Dogmas of Empiricism", in his *From a Logical Point of View* (New York: Harper and Row, 1961), pp.20-46. Historical accounts of the Copernican Revolution that poses difficulties for falsificationists are in T. Kuhn, *The Copernican Revolution* (New York: Random House, 1959); A. Koyré, *Metaphysics and Measurement* (London: Chapman and Hall, 1968); and P.K. Feyerabend, *Against Method: Outline of an Anarchistic Theory of Knowledge* (London: New Left Books, 1975). Lakatos's article, "Popper on Demarcation and Induction", in *The Philosophy of Karl R. Popper,* ed. P.A. Schilpp (La Salle, Illinois: Open Court, 1974), is critical of the falsificationist claim to have solved the problem of induction. Kuhn criticizes falsificationism in *The Structure of Scientific Revolutions* (Chicago: Chicago University Press, 1970) and in "Logic of Discovery of Psychology of Research?", in *Criticism and the Growth of Knowledge,* ed. Lakatos and Musgrave, pp.1-23.

1. K.R. Popper, *The Logic of Scientific Discovery* (London: Hutchinson, 1968), p.106.
2. Ibid., p.99.
3. Ibid., p.111.
4. I. Lakatos, "Falsification and the Methodology of Scientific Research Programmes", in *Criticism and the Growth of Knowledge,* ed. I. Lakatos and A. Musgrave (Cambridge: Cambridge University Press, 1974), p.100-101.
5. Ibid., p.140-54.
6. J.C. Maxwell, "Illustrations of the Dynamical Theory of Gases", read before the British Association in 1859 and reprinted in *The Scientific Papers of James Clerk Maxwell,* 2 vols., ed. W.D. Niven (New York: Dover, 1965), vol.1, pp.377-409. See especially the final paragraph of the paper.

7. J.C. Maxwell, "The Kinetic Theory of Gases", *Nature* 16 (1877): 245-46.
8. My remarks on Galileo and the telescope, and several other aspects of my estimate of Galileo's physics stem from Feyerabend's provocative account in *Against Method: Outline of an Anarchistic Theory of Knowledge,* (London: New Left Books, 1975), pp.69-164.
9. Galileo Galilei, *Two New Sciences,* trans. Stillman Drake (Madison: University of Wisconsin Press, 1974).

7

Theories as Structures:
1. Research Programmes

1. Theories should be considered as structural wholes

The sketch of the Copernican Revolution presented in the previous chapter strongly suggests that the inductivist and falsificationist accounts of science are too piecemeal. Concentrating on the relationships between theories and individual observation statements or sets of them, they fail to take account of the complexity of major scientific theories. Neither the naive inductivist emphasis on the inductive derivation of theories from observation, nor the falsificationist scheme of conjectures and falsifications, is capable of yielding an adequate characterization of the genesis and growth of realistically complex theories. More adequate pictures involve the depiction of theories as structured wholes of some kind.

One reason why it is necessary to regard theories as structures stems from a study of the history of science. Historical study reveals that the evolution and progress of major sciences exhibit a structure that is not captured by the inductivist or falsificationist accounts. The programmatic development of the Copernican theory over more than a century has already provided us with one example. Later in this chapter we will meet others. However, the historical argument is not the only ground for the claim that theories are structural wholes of some kind. Another more general philosophical argument is closely linked with the theory-dependence of observation. It was stressed in Chapter 3 that observation statements must be formulated in the language of some theory. Consequently, the statements, and the concepts figuring in them, will be as precise and informative as the theory in whose language they are framed is precise and informative. For example, I think it will be agreed that the Newtonian concept of mass has a more precise meaning than the concept of democracy, say. I suggest that the reason for the relatively precise meaning of the former stems from the fact that the concept plays a specific, well-defined role in a precise, structured theory, Newtonian mechanics. By contrast, the theories in which the concept "democracy" occurs are notoriously vague and multifarious. If this suggested close connection, between precision of meaning of a term or statement and the role played by that term or statement is a theory, is valid, then the need for coherently structured theories follows fairly directly from it.

The dependence of the meaning of concepts on the structure of the theory in which they occur, and the dependence of the precision of the former on the precision and degree of coherence of the latter, can be made more plausible by noting the limitations of some alternative ways in which a concept might be thought to acquire meaning. One such alternative is the view that concepts acquire their meaning by way of a *definition*. Definitions must be rejected as a fundamental procedure for establishing meanings. Concepts can only be defined in terms of other concepts, the meanings of which are given. If the meanings of these latter concepts are themselves established by definition, it is clear that an infinite regress will result unless the meanings of some terms are known by some other means. A dictionary is useless unless one already knows the meanings of many words. Newton could not *define* mass or force in terms of pre-Newtonian concepts. It was necessary for him to transcend the terms of the old conceptual system by developing a new one. A second alternative is the suggestion that the meaning of concepts is established through observation, by way of *ostensive definition*. A central difficulty with this suggestion has already been discussed in connection with the concept "red" on p.29. One will not arrive at the concept "mass" through observation alone, however closely one scrutinizes colliding billiard-balls, weights on springs, orbiting planets, etc., nor is it possible to teach others the meaning of mass merely by pointing to such events. It is not irrelevant to recall here that if one attempts to teach a dog by way of ostensive definition, it invariably responds by sniffing one's finger.

The claim that concepts derive their meaning at least in part from the role they play in a theory is supported by the following historical reflections.

Contrary to the popular myth, Galileo seems to have performed few experiments in mechanics. Many of the "experiments" he refers to while articulating his theory are thought experiments. This is a paradoxical fact for those empiricists who think that new theories are derived from the facts in some way, but it is quite comprehensible when it is realized that precise experimentation can only be carried out if one has a precise theory capable of yielding predictions in the form of precise observation statements. Galileo was in the process of making a major contribution to the building of a new mechanics that was to prove capable of supporting detailed experimentation at a later stage. It need not be surprising that his efforts involved thought experiments, analogies and illustrative metaphors rather than detailed experimentation. I suggest that the typical history of a concept, whether it be "chemical element", "atom", "the unconscious", or whatever, involves the initial emergence of the concept as a vague idea, followed by its gradual clarification as the theory in which it plays a part takes a more precise and coherent form. The emergence of the concept of electric field provides a particularly striking, if somewhat technical, example. When the concept was first introduced by Faraday in the fourth decade of the nineteenth century it was very vague, and was articulated with the aid of mechanical analogies and a metaphorical use of terms such as "tension", "power" and "force". The field concept became increasingly better defined as the relationships between the electric field and other electromagnetic quantities were more clearly specified. Once Maxwell had introduced his displacement current it was possible to bring great coherence to the theory in the form of Maxwell's equations, which clearly established the inter-relationship between all the electromagnetic field quantities. It was at this stage that the meaning of "electric field" in classical electromagnetic theory reached a high degree of clarity and precision. It was at this stage, too, that the fields were granted an independence of their own and the aether, which had been considered necessary for providing a mechanical basis for the fields, was dispensed with.

So far we have mentioned two reasons why theories must be seen as organized structures of some kind: the fact that historical study shows theories to possess that feature and the fact that it is only by way of a coherently structured theory that concepts acquire a precise meaning. A third reason stems from the need for science to grow. It is clear that science will advance more efficiently if theories are so structured as to contain within them fairly clear clues and prescriptions as to how they should be developed and extended. They should be open-ended structures that offer a research *programme*. Newton's mechanics provided such a programme for eighteenth and nineteenth-century physicists, the programme for explaining the entire physical world in terms of mechanical systems involving various forces and governed by Newton's laws of motion. This coherent programme might be compared with modern sociology, much of which is sufficiently concerned with empirical data to satisfy the falsificationist if not the inductivist criteria of good science and yet fails miserably to emulate the success of physics. I suggest, following Lakatos, that the crucial difference lies in the relative coherence of the two theories. Modern sociological theories fail to spell out a coherent programme to guide future research.

2. Lakatos's research programmes

The remainder of the chapter will be devoted to a summary of one notable attempt to analyze theories as organized structures, Imre Lakatos's "Methodology of Scientific Research Programmes".[1] Lakatos developed his picture of science in an attempt to improve on, and overcome the objections to, Popperian falsificationism.

A Lakatosian research programme is a structure that provides guidance for future research in both a positive and a negative way. The *negative heuristic* of a programme involves the stipulation that the basic assumptions underlying the programme, its *hard core,* must not be rejected or modified. It is protected from falsification by a *protective belt* of auxiliary hypotheses, initial conditions, etc. The *positive heuristic* is comprised of rough guidelines indicating how the research programme might be developed. Such development will involve supplementing the hard core with additional assumptions in an attempt to account for previously known phenomena and to predict novel phenomena. Research programmes will be *progressive* or *degenerating* depending on whether they succeed in leading or whether they persistently fail to lead to the discovery of novel phenomena. Lest the reader be discouraged by this barrage of new terminology, let me hasten to explain it in fairly simple terms.

The hard core of a programme is, more than anything else, the defining characteristic of a programme. It takes the form of some very general theoretical hypotheses that form the basis from which the programme is to develop. Here are some examples. The hard core of Copernican astronomy would be the assumptions that the earth and the planets orbit a stationary sun and that the earth spins on its axis once a day. The hard core of Newtonian physics is comprised of Newton's laws of motion plus his law of gravitional attraction. The hard core of Marx's historical materialism would be the assumption that social change is to be explained in terms of class struggle, the nature of the classes and the details of the struggle being determined in the last instance by the economic base.

The hard core of a programme is rendered unfalsifiable by "the methodological decision of its protagonists".[2] Any inadequacy in the match between an articulated research programme and observational data is to be attributed, not to assumptions that constitute the hard core, but to some other part of the theoretical structure. The maze of assumptions that constitute this other part of the structure is what Lakatos refers to as the protective belt. It consists not only of explicit auxiliary hypotheses supplementing the hard core but also assumptions underlying the description of the initial conditions and also observation statements. For example, the hard core of the Copernican research programme needed to be augmented by adding numerous epicycles to the initially circular planetary orbits and it was also necessary to change the previously accepted estimate of the distance of the stars from earth. If observed planetary behaviour differed from that predicted by the Copernican research programme at some stage in its development then the hard core of the programme could be protected by modifying the epicycles or adding new ones. Eventually other, initially implicit, assumptions were to be unearthed and modified. The hard core was protected by changing the theory underlying the observation language, so that telescopic data replaced naked-eye observations, for instance. The initial conditions also came to be modified eventually, with the addition of new planets.

The negative heuristic of a programme is the demand that during the development of the programme the hard core is to remain unmodified and intact. Any scientist who modifies the hard core has opted out of that particular research programme. Tycho Brahé opted out of the Copernican research programme and initiated another when he proposed that all planets other than the earth orbit the sun, while the sun itself orbits a stationary earth. Lakatos's emphasis on the conventional element attached to work within a research programme, on the need for scientists to *decide* to accept its hard core, has much in common with Popper's position with respect to observation statements, which was discussed in section 2 of the previous chapter. The major difference is that whereas in Popper the decisions concern the acceptance of singular statements only, in Lakatos the device is extended so as to be applicable to the *universal* statements that make up the hard core. I have similar reservations about Lakatos's emphasis on the explicit decisions of individual scientists to those I mentioned in connection with Popper. The question will be discussed more fully in later chapters.

The positive heuristic, that aspect of a research programme that indicates to scientists the kind of thing they should do rather than what they should not do, is somewhat vaguer and more difficult to characterize specifically than the negative heuristic. The positive heuristic indicates how the hard core is to be supplemented in order for it to be capable of explaining and predicting real phenomena. In Lakatos's own words, "The positive heuristic consists of a partially articulated set of suggestions or hints on how to change, develop, the 'refutable variants' of the research programme, how to modify, sophisticate, the 'refutable' protective belt".[3] The development of a research programme will involve not only the addition of suitable auxiliary hypotheses but also the development of adequate mathematical and experimental techniques. For instance, from the very inception of the Copernican programme it was clear that adequate mathematical techniques for manipulating epicyclic motions, improved techniques for astronomical observations and adequate theories governing the use of a variety of instruments were necessary for the elaboration and detailed application of the programme.

Lakatos illustrated the notion of the positive heuristic with the story of Newton's early development of his gravitational theory.[4] Newton first arrived at the inverse square law of attraction by considering the elliptical motion of a point planet around a stationary point sun. It was clear that if the gravitational theory was to be applied in practice to planetary motion, the programme would need to develop from this idealized model to more realistic ones. But that development involved the solution of theoretical problems and was not to be achieved without considerable theoretical labour. Newton himself, faced with a definite programme, that is, guided by a positive heuristic, made considerable progress. He first took into account the fact that a sun as well as a planet moves under the influence of their mutual attraction. Then he took account of the finite size of the planets and treated them as spheres. After solving the mathematical problem posed by that move, Newton proceeded to allow for other complications such as those introduced by the possibility that a planet can spin, and the fact that there are gravitational forces between the individual planets as well as between each planet and the sun. When Newton had progressed that far in the programme, following a path that had presented itself as more or less necessary from the outset, he began to be concerned about the match between his theory and observation. When the match was found wanting, he was able to proceed to non-spherical planets, and so on. As well as the theoretical programme contained in the positive heuristic, a fairly definite experimental programme suggested itself. That programme included the development of more accurate telescopes, together with auxiliary theories required for their use in astronomy such as those providing adequate means for allowing for refraction of light in the earth's atmosphere. The initial formulation of Newton's programme also implied the desirability of constructing apparatus sensitive enough to detect gravitional attraction on a laboratory scale (Cavendish's experiment).

The programme implicit in Newton's gravitational theory gave strong heuristic guidance. Lakatos gives a fairly detailed account of Bohr's theory of the atom as another convincing example.[5] An important feature of these examples of developing research programmes is the comparatively late stage at which observational testing becomes relevant. This is in keeping with my comments about Galileo's construction of the origins of mechanics in the previous section. Early work on a research programme takes place without heed of or in spite of apparent falsifications by observation. A research programme must be given a chance to realize its full potential. A suitably sophisticated and adequate protective belt must be constructed. In our example of the Copernican Revolution, this included the development of an adequate mechanics and optics. When a programme has been developed to a stage where it is appropriate to subject it to observational tests it is confirmations rather than falsifications that are of paramount importance, according to Lakatos.[6] A research programme is required to succeed, at least intermittently, to make novel predictions that turn out to be confirmed. The notion of a "novel" prediction was discussed in section 4 of Chapter 5. Newton's theory experienced dramatic successes of this kind when Galle first observed the planet Neptune and Cavendish first detected gravitational attraction on the laboratory scale. Such successes were the marks of the progressive character of the programme. By contrast, Ptolemaic astronomy had failed to predict novel phenomena throughout the Middle Ages. By Newton's time, the Ptolemaic theory was decidedly a degenerating one.

Two ways in which the merit of a research programme is to be assessed have emerged from the foregoing outline. Firstly, a research programme should possess a degree of coherence that involves the mapping out of a definite programme for future research. Secondly, a research programme should lead to the discovery of novel phenomena at least occasionally. A research programme must satisfy both conditions if it is to qualify as a scientific one. Lakatos offers Marxism and Freudian psychology as programmes that satisfy the first criterion but do not satisfy the second, and modern sociology as a programme that perhaps satisfies the second but does not satisfy the first.

3. Methodology within a research programme

Within Lakatos's framework, scientific methodology must be discussed from two points of view, one concerning the work done within a single research programme, the other concerning the comparison of the merits of competing research programmes. Work within a single research programme involves the expansion and modification of its protective belt by the addition and articulation of various hypotheses. What kinds of additions and modifications are to be permitted by a good scientific methodology and what kinds are to be ruled out as non-scientific? Lakatos's answer to this question is straightforward. Any move is permissable as long as it is not *ad hoc*, in the sense discussed in section 2 of Chapter 5. Modifications or additions to the protective belt of a research programme must be independently testable. Individual scientists or groups of scientists are invited to develop the protective belt in any way they choose, provided their moves offer the opportunity of fresh tests and hence the possibility of new discoveries. By way of illustration, let us take an example from the development of Newton's theory that we have considered several times before, and consider the situation that confronted Leverrier and Adams when they addressed themselves to the troublesome orbit of the planet Uranus. Those scientists chose to modify the protective belt of the programme by proposing that the initial conditions were inadequate. Their detailed proposal was scientific because it was independently testable, and, as it eventuated, led to the discovery of the planet Neptune. But other possible responses to the problem would be genuinely scientific on Lakatos' account. Another scientist might have proposed a modification in the optical theory governing the operation of the telescopes used in the investigation. This move would have been scientific if, for example, it had involved the prediction of a new kind of aberration in such a way that the existence of the new aberration could be tested by optical experiments. Another move might have involved challenging some assumption in the protective belt such as those concerning refraction in the earth's atmosphere. Such a move would have been legitimate if it had offered the possibility of new kinds of experimental tests, perhaps leading to the discovery of some unexpected feature of the earth's atmosphere.

Two kinds of move are ruled out by Lakatos's methodology. *Ad hoc* hypotheses, hypotheses that are not independently testable, are ruled out. For instance, in our example, it would have been unscientific to propose that the troublesome motion of the planet Uranus was such because that was its natural motion. The other kind of move that is ruled out is one that violates the hard core, as we have already mentioned. A scientist who tried to cope with the orbit of Uranus by proposing that the force between Uranus and the sun obeyed something other than the inverse square law would be opting out of the Newtonian research programme.

The fact that any part of a complex theoretical maze might be responsible for an apparent falsification poses a serious problem for the falsificationist relying on an unqualified method of conjectures and refutations. For him, the inability to locate the source of the trouble resulted in unmethodical chaos. Lakatos's account of science is sufficiently structured to avoid that consequence. Order is maintained by the inviolability of the hard core of a programme and by the positive heuristic that accompanies it. The proliferation of ingenious conjectures within that framework will lead to progress provided some of the predictions resulting from the ingenious conjectures occasionally prove successful. Decisions to retain or reject an hypothesis are fairly straightforwardly determined by the results of experimental tests. Those that survive experimental tests are provisionally retained and those that fail to survive them are rejected, although some decisions are open to appeal in the light of some further ingenious, independently testable hypothesis. The bearing of observation on an hypothesis under test is relatively unproblematic within a research programme because the hard core and the positive heuristic serve to define a fairly stable observation language.

4. The comparison of research programmes

While the relative merits of competing hypotheses within a research programme can be determined in a relatively straightforward way, the comparison of rival research programmes is more problematic. Roughly speaking, the relative merits of research programmes are to be judged by the extent to which they are progressing or degenerating. A degenerating programme will give way to a more progressive rival, just as Ptolemaic astronomy eventually gave way to the Copernican theory.

A major difficulty with this criterion for the acceptance and rejection of research programmes is associated with the time factor. How much time must elapse before it can be decided that a programme has seriously degenerated, that it is incapable of leading to the discovery of new phenomena? Lakatos's parable about hypothetical planetary misbehaviour, reproduced on pp.65-66, indicates the difficulty. In this imaginary development within Newtonian astronomy, it was never possible to be sure that a major success was not just around the corner. To take a genuine historical example, it was over seventy years before Copernicus's prediction about the phases of Venus was found to be correct, and several centuries before the Copernican prediction that the fixed stars should exhibit parallax was confirmed. Because of the uncertainty of the outcome of future attempts to develop and test a research programme, it can never be said of any programme that it has degenerated beyond all hope. It is always possible that some ingenious modification of its protective belt will lead to some spectacular discovery that will bring the programme to life again and set it on a progressive phase.

The history of theories of electricity provides an example of the changing fortunes of rival research programmes. One programme, which I will call the action at a distance theory, regarded electricity as a fluid or particles of some kind residing in electrically charged bodies and flowing through electrical circuits. Separated elements of electricity were supposed to act on each other instantaneously at a distance across empty space with a force depending on the separation and the motion of the elements. The other programme was the field theory initiated by Faraday, according to which electrical phenomena can be explained in terms of actions going on in the medium surrounding electrified bodies and electric circuits, rather than in terms of the behaviour of a substance within them. Before Faraday's successes it was the action at a distance theory that was progressive. It led to the discovery of the ability of a Leyden jar to store electricity and to Cavendish's discovery of the inverse square law of attraction or repulsion between charged bodies. However, the field approach was to surpass the action at a distance approach with Faraday's discovery of electromagnetic induction and his invention of the electric motor, the dynamo and the transformer in the 1830s. The field theory progressed even more dramatically when, a few decades later, Hertz produced the radio waves predicted by the programme. Nevertheless, the action at a distance theory was not finished. It was from that programme that the notion of the electron emerged. It had been predicted in a vague form by action at a distance theorist W. Weber in the first half of the nineteenth century, was predicted in a more precise way by H.A. Lorentz in 1892, and was eventually detected experimentally by J.J. Thomson and others later that decade. The development of classical electromagnetic theory would have been much impaired if the action at a distance approach had been abandoned earlier in the century because of the superior progress of the field programme. Incidentally, the interaction between the two programmes, and the fact that classical electromagnetic theory emerged as a reconciliation of the two programmes, inheriting the fields from one and the electron from the other, suggests that research programmes are not as autonomous as the Lakatos account suggests.

Within the Lakatos account, then, one can never make the unqualified claim that one research programme is "better" than a rival. Lakatos himself admits that the relative merits of two programmes can only be decided "with hindsight". Because he has failed to offer a clear-cut criterion for the rejection of any coherent research programme, or for choosing between rival research programmes, one might wish to say, with Feyerabend, that Lakatos's methodology is "a *verbal ornament,* as a memorial to happier times when it was still thought possible to run a complex and often catastrophic business like science by following a few simple and 'rational' rules".[7] The issue raised here will be discussed in some detail in Chapter 9.

FURTHER READING

The key source is I. Lakatos, "Falsification and the Methodology of Scientific Research Programmes", in *Criticism and the Growth of Knowledge,* ed. I. Lakatos and A. Musgrave (Cambridge: Cambridge University Press,

1974), pp.91-196. Some historical case-studies from the Lakatos viewpoint are E. Zahar, "Why Did Einstein's Programme Supersede Lorentz's?", in *British Journal for the Philosophy of Science* 24 (1973): 95-123, 223-63; I. Lakatos and E. Zahar, "Why Did Copernicus's Programme Supersede Ptolemy's?", in *The Copernican Achievement,* ed. R. Westman (Berkeley, Calif.: California University Press, 1975); and the studies in Colin Howson, ed., *Method and Appraisal in the Physical Sciences* (Cambridge: Cambridge University Press, 1976). Most of Lakatos's papers have been collected and published in two volumes edited by John Worrall and Gregory Currie (Cambridge: Cambridge University Press, 1978). The extent to which Lakatos's research programmes are self-contained is criticized in Noretta Koertge, "Inter-theoretic Criticism and the Growth of Science", in *Boston Studies in Philosophy of Science,* vol. 8, ed. R.C. Buck and R.S. Cohen (Dordrecht: Reidel Publ. Co., 1971), pp.160-73. The positions of Lakatos and Kuhn are compared, and Kuhn defended, in D. Bloor, "Two Paradigms of Scientific Knowledge?", *Science Studies* 1 (1971): 101-15. The notion of a novel prediction is pursued by Alan E. Musgrave, "Logical Versus Historical Theories of Confirmation", *British Journal for the Philosophy of Science* 25 (1974): 1-23.

1. I. Lakatos, "Falsification and the Methodology of Scientific Research Programmes", in *Criticism and the Growth of Knowledge,* ed. I. Lakatos and A. Musgrave (Cambridge: Cambridge University Press, 1974), pp.91-196.
2. Ibid., p.133.
3. Ibid., p.135.
4. Ibid., pp.145-46.
5. Ibid., pp.140-54.
6. I here use "confirmation" in the same way as in earlier chapters to refer to results of an experimental test that turn out to support a theory, rather than to the proof of a theory. Lakatos used "verification" where I have used "confirmation".
7. P.K. Feyerabend, "Consolations for the Specialist", in *Criticism and the Growth of Knowledge,* ed. Lakatos and Musgrave, p.215.

8

Theories as Structures:
2. Kuhn's Paradigms

1. Introductory remarks

A second view that a scientific theory is a complex structure of some kind is one that has received a great deal of attention in recent years. I refer to the view developed by Thomas Kuhn, the first version of which appeared in his book *The Structure of Scientific Revolutions,* initially published in 1962.[1] Kuhn started his academic career as a physicist and then turned his attention to history of science. On doing so, he found that his preconceptions about the nature of science were shattered. He came to realize that traditional accounts of science, whether inductivisit or falsificationist, do not bear comparison with historical evidence. Kuhn's theory of science was subsequently developed as an attempt to give a theory of science more in keeping with the historical situation as he saw it. A key feature of his theory is the emphasis placed on the revolutionary character of scientific progress, where a revolution involves the abandonment of one theoretical structure and its replacement by another, incompatible one. Another important feature is the important role played in Kuhn's theory by the sociological characteristics of scientific communities.

The approaches of Lakatos and Kuhn have some things in common. In particular, both demand of their philosophical accounts that they stand up to criticism based on the history of science. Kuhn's account predates Lakatos's methodology of scientific research programmes, and I think it is fair to say that Lakatos adapted some of Kuhn's results to his own purposes. Lakatos's account was presented first in this book because it is best seen as a culmination of the Popperian programme and as a direct response to and an attempt to improve on the limitations of Popperian falsificationism. The major differences between Kuhn on the one hand and Popper and Lakatos on the other is the former's emphasis on sociological factors. Kuhn's "relativism" will be discussed and criticized later in the book. In the present chapter, I will restrict myself to a simple summary of Kuhn's views.

Kuhn's picture of the way a science progresses can be summarized by the following open-ended scheme:

pre-science — normal science — crisis-revolution — new normal science — new crisis

The disorganized and diverse activity that precedes the formation of a science eventually becomes structured and directed when a single *paradigm* becomes adhered to by a scientific community. A paradigm is made up of the general theoretical assumptions and laws and techniques for their application that the members of a particular scientific community adopt. Workers within a paradigm, whether it be Newtonian mechanics, wave optics, analytical chemistry or whatever, practise what Kuhn calls *normal science*. Normal scientists will articulate and develop the paradigm in their attempt to account for and accommodate the behaviour of some relevant aspects of the real world as revealed through the results of experimentation. In doing so, they will inevitably experience difficulties and encounter apparent falsifications. If difficulties of that kind get out of hand, a *crisis* state develops. A crisis is resolved when an entirely new paradigm emerges and attracts the allegiance of more and more scientists until eventually the original, problem-ridden paradigm is abandoned. The discontinuous change constitutes a *scientific revolution*. The new paradigm, full of promise and not beset by apparently insuperable difficulties, now guides new normal scientific activity until it too runs into serious trouble and a new crisis followed by a new revolution results.

With this résumé as a foretaste, let us proceed to look at the various components of Kuhn's scheme in more detail.

2. Paradigms and normal science

A mature science is governed by a single paradigm.[2] The paradigm sets the standards for legitimate work within the science it governs. It co-ordinates and directs the "puzzle-solving" activity of the groups of normal scientists that work within it. The existence of a paradigm capable of supporting a normal science tradition is the characteristic that distinguishes science from non-science, according to Kuhn. Newtonian mechanics, wave optics and classical electromagnetism all constituted and perhaps constitute paradigms and qualify as sciences. Much of modern sociology lacks a paradigm and consequently fails to qualify as science.

As will be explained below, it is of the nature of a paradigm to belie precise definition. Nevertheless, it is possible to describe some of the typical components that go to make up a paradigm. Among the components will be explicitly stated laws and theoretical assumptions comparable to the components of the hard core of a Lakatosian research programme. Thus Newton's laws of motion form part of the Newtonian paradigm and Maxwell's equations form part of the paradigm that constitutes classical electromagnetic theory. Paradigms will also include standard ways of applying the fundamental laws to a variety of types of situation. For instance, the Newtonian paradigm will include methods of applying Newton's laws to planetary motion, pendulums, billiard-ball collisions, and so on. Instrumentation and instrumental techniques necessary for bringing the laws of the paradigm to bear on the real world will also be included in the paradigm. The application of the Newtonian paradigm in astronomy involves the use of a variety of approved kinds of telescope, together with techniques for their use and a variety of techniques for the correction of the data collected with their aid. A further component of paradigms consists of some very general, metaphysical principles that guide work within a paradigm. Throughout the nineteenth century, the Newtonian paradigm was governed by an assumption something like, "The whole of the physical world is to be explained as a mechanical system operating under the influence of various forces according to the dictates of Newton's laws of motion", and the Cartesian programme in the seventeenth century involved the principle, "There is no void and the physical universe is a big clockwork in which all forces take the form of a push". Finally, all paradigms will contain some very general methodological prescriptions such as, "Make serious attempts to match your paradigm with nature", or "Treat failures in attempts to match a paradigm with nature as serious problems".

Normal science involves detailed attempts to articulate a paradigm with the aim of improving the match between it and nature. A paradigm will always be sufficiently imprecise and open-ended to leave plenty of that kind of work to be done.[3] Kuhn portrays normal science as a puzzle-solving activity governed by the rules of a paradigm. The puzzles will be of both a theoretical and experimental nature. Within the Newtonian paradigm, for instance, typical theoretical puzzles involve devising mathematical techniques for dealing with the motion of a planet subject to more than one attractive force, and developing assumptions suitable for applying Newton's laws to the motion of fluids. Experimental puzzles included the improvement of the accuracy of telescopic observations and the development of experimental techniques capable of yielding reliable measurements of the gravititional constant. Normal scientists must presuppose that a paradigm provides the means for the solution of the puzzles posed within it. A failure to solve a puzzle is seen as a failure of the scientist rather than as an inadequacy of the paradigm. Puzzles that resist solution are seen as *anomalies* rather than as falsifications of a paradigm. Kuhn recognizes that all paradigms will contain some anomalies (e.g. the Copernican theory and the apparent size of Venus or the Newtonian paradigm and the orbit of Mercury) and rejects all brands of falsificationism.

A normal scientist must be uncritical of the paradigm in which he works. It is only by being so that he is able to concentrate his efforts on the detailed articulation of the paradigm and to perform the esoteric work necessary to probe nature in depth. It is the lack of disagreement over fundamentals that distinguishes mature, normal science from the relatively disorganized activity of immature *pre-science*. According to Kuhn, the latter is characterized by total disagreement and constant debate over fundamentals, so much so that it is impossible to get down to detailed, esoteric work. There will be almost as many theories as there are workers in the field and each theoretician will be obliged to start afresh and justify his own particular approach. Kuhn offers optics before Newton as an example. There was a wide diversity of theories about the nature of light from the time of the ancients up to Newton. No general agreement was reached and no detailed, generally accepted theory emerged before Newton proposed and defended his particle theory. Not only did the rival theorists of the pre-science period disagree over fundamental theoretical assumptions but also over the kinds of observational phenomena that were relevant to their theories. Insofar as Kuhn recognizes the role played by a paradigm in guiding the search for and interpretation of observable phenomena, he accommodates most of what I have described as the theory-dependence of observation in Chapter 3.

Kuhn insists that there is more to a paradigm that can be explicitly laid down in the form of explicit rules and directions. He invokes Wittgenstein's discussion of the notion "game" to illustrate some of what he means. Wittgenstein argued that it is not possible to spell out necessary and sufficient conditions for an activity to be a game. When one tries, one invariably finds an activity that one's definition includes but that one would not want to count as a game, or an activity that the definition excludes but that one would want to count as a game. Kuhn claims that the same situation exists with respect to paradigms. If one tries to give a precise and explicit characterization of some paradigm in the history of science or in present-day science, it always turns out that some work within the paradigm violates the characterization. However, Kuhn insists that this state of affairs does not render the concept of paradigm untenable any more than the similar situation with respect to "game" rules out legitimate use of that concept. Even though there is no complete, explicit characterization, individual scientists acquire knowledge of a paradigm through their scientific education. By solving standard problems, performing standard experiments and eventually by doing a piece of research under a supervisor already a skilled practitioner within the paradigm, an aspiring scientist becomes acquainted with the methods, the techniques and the standards of that paradigm. He will be no more able to give an explicit account of the methods and skills he has acquired than a master-carpenter will be able to fully describe what lies behind his skills. Much of the normal scientist's knowledge will be *tacit*, in the sense developed by Michael Polanyi.[4]

Because of the way he is trained, and needs to be trained if he is to work efficiently, a typical normal scientist will be unaware of and unable to articulate the precise nature of the paradigm in which he works. However, it does not follow from this that a scientist will not be able to attempt to articulate the presuppositions involved in his paradigm, should the need arise. Such a need will arise when a paradigm is threatened by a rival. In those circumstances, it will be necessary to attempt to spell out the general laws, metaphysical and methodological principles, etc. involved in a paradigm in order to defend them against the alternatives involved in the threatening new paradigm. In the next section, I proceed to summarize Kuhn's account of how a paradigm can run into trouble and be replaced by a rival.

3. Crisis and revolution

The normal scientist works confidently within a well-defined area dictated by a paradigm. The paradigm presents him with a set of definite problems together with methods that he is confident will be adequate for their solution. If he blames the paradigm for any failure to solve a problem, he will be open to the same charges as the carpenter who blames his tools. Nevertheless, failures will be encountered and such failures can eventually attain a degree of seriousness that constitutes a serious crisis for the paradigm and may lead to the rejection of a paradigm and its replacement by an incompatible alternative.

The mere existence of unsolved puzzles within a paradigm does not constitute a crisis. Kuhn recognizes that paradigms will always encounter difficulties. There will always be anomalies. It is only under special sets of conditions that the anomalies can develop in such a way as to undermine confidence in the paradigm. An anomaly will be regarded as particularly serious if it is seen as striking at the very fundamentals of a paradigm and yet persistently resists attempts by the members of the normal scientific community to remove it. Kuhn cites as an example problems associated with the aether and the earth's motion relative to it in Maxwell's electromagnetic theory, towards the end of the nineteenth century. A less-technical example would be the problems that comets posed for the ordered and full Aristotelian cosmos of interconnected crystalline spheres. Anomalies are also regarded as serious if they are important with respect to some pressing social need. The problems that beset Ptolemaic astronomy were pressing ones in the light of the need for calendar reform at the time of Copernicus. Also bearing on the seriousness of an anomaly will be the length of time that it resists attempts to remove it. The number of serious anomalies is a further factor influencing the onset of a crisis.

According to Kuhn, an analysis of the characteristics of a crisis period in science demands the competence of the psychologist as much as that of an historian. When anomalies come to be seen as posing serious problems for a paradigm, a period of "pronounced professional insecurity" sets in.[5] Attempts to solve the problem become more and more radical and the rules set by the paradigm for the solution of problems become progressively more loosened. Normal scientists begin to engage in philosophical and metaphysical disputes and try to defend their innovations, of dubious status from the point of view of the paradigm, by philosophical arguments. Scientists even begin to express openly their discontent with and unease over the reigning paradigm. Kuhn quotes Wolfgang Pauli's response to what he saw as the growing crisis in physics around 1924. An exasperated Pauli confessed to a friend, "At the moment, physics is again terribly confused. In any case, it is too difficult for me, and I wish I had been a movie comedian or something of the sort and had never heard of physics".[6] Once a paradigm has been weakened and undermined to such an extent that its proponents lose their confidence in it, the time is ripe for revolution.

The seriousness of a crisis deepens when a rival paradigm makes its appearance. "The new paradigm, or a sufficient hint to permit later articulation, emerges all at once, sometimes in the middle of the night, in the mind of a man deeply immersed in crisis".[7] The new paradigm will be very different from and incompatible with the old one. The radical differences will be of a variety of kinds.

Each paradigm will regard the world as being made up of different kinds of things. The Aristotelian paradigm saw the universe as divided into two distinct realms, the incorruptible and unchanging super-lunar region and the corruptible and changing earthly region. Later paradigms saw the entire universe as being made up of the same kinds of material substances. Pre-Lavoisier chemistry involved the claim that the world contained a substance called phlogiston, which is driven from materials when they are burnt. Lavoisier's new paradigm implied that there is no such thing as phlogiston, whereas the gas, oxygen, does exist and plays a quite different role in combustion. Maxwell's electromagnetic theory involved an aether occupying all space, whereas Einstein's radical recasting of it eliminated the aether.

Rival paradigms will regard different kinds of questions as legitimate or meaningful. Questions about the weight of phlogiston were important for phlogiston theorists and vacuous for Lavoisier. Questions about the mass of planets were fundamental for Newtonians and heretical for Aristotelians. The problem of the velocity of the earth relative to the aether, which was deeply significant for pre-Einsteinian physicists, was dissolved by Einstein. As well as posing different kinds of questions, paradigms will involve different and incompatible standards. Unexplained action at a distance was permitted by Newtonians but dismissed by Cartesians as metaphysical and even occult. Uncaused motion was nonsense for Aristotle and axiomatic for Newton. The transmutation of elements has an important place in modern nuclear physics (as it did in mediaeval alchemy) but ran completely counter to the aims of Dalton's atomistic programme. A number of kinds of events describable within modern microphysics involve an indeterminancy that had no place in the Newtonian programme.

The way a scientist views a particular aspect of the world will be guided by a paradigm in which he is working. Kuhn argues that there is a sense in which proponents of rival paradigms are "living in different worlds". He cites as evidence the fact that changes in the heavens were first noted, recorded and discussed by Western astronomers after the proposal of the Copernican theory. Before that, the Aristotelian paradigm had dictated that there could be no change in the super-lunar region and, accordingly, no change was observed. Those changes that were noticed were explained away as disturbances in the upper atmosphere. More of Kuhn's examples, and others besides, have already been given in Chapter 3.

The change of allegiance on the part of individual scientists from one paradigm to an incompatible alternative is likened by Kuhn to a "gestalt switch" or a "religious conversion". There will be no purely logical argument that demonstrates the superiority of one paradigm over another and that thereby compels a rational scientist to make the change. One reason why no such demonstration is possible is the fact that a variety of factors are involved in a scientist's judgement of the merits of a scientific theory. An individual scientist's decision will depend on the priority he gives to the various factors. The factors will include such things as simplicity, the connection with some pressing social need, the ability to solve some specified kind of problem, and so on. Thus one scientist might be attracted to the Copernican theory because of the simplicity of certain mathematical features of it. Another might be attracted to it because he sees in it the possibility of calendar reform. A third might have been deterred from adopting the Copernican theory because of his involvement with terrestrial mechanics and his awareness of the problems that the Copernican theory posed for it. A fourth might reject Copernicanism for religious reasons.

A second reason why no logically compelling demonstration of the superiority of one paradigm over another exists stems from the fact that proponents of rival paradigms will subscribe to different sets of standards, metaphysical principles, etc. Judged by its own standards, paradigm A may be judged superior to paradigm B, while if the standards of paradigm B are used as premises, the judgement may be reversed. The conclusion of an argument is compelling only if its premises are accepted. Supporters of rival paradigms will not accept each other's premises and so will not necessarily be convinced by each other's arguments. It is for this kind of reason that Kuhn compares scientific revolutions to political revolutions. Just as "political revolutions aim to change politicial institutions in ways that those institutions themselves prohibit" and consequently "political recourse fails", so the choice "between competing paradigms proves to be a choice between incompatible modes of community life", and no argument can be "logically or even probabilistically compelling".[8] This is not to say, however, that various arguments will not be among the important factors that influence the decisions of scientists. On Kuhn's view, the kinds of factors that do prove effective in causing scientists to change paradigms is a matter to be discovered by psychological and sociological investigation.

There are a number of interrelated reasons, then, why, when one paradigm competes with another; there is no logically compelling argument that dictates that a rational scientist should abandon one for the other. There is no single criterion by which a scientist must judge the merit or promise of a paradigm, and further, proponents of competing programmes will subscribe to different sets of standards and will even view the world in different ways and describe it in a different language. The aim of arguments and discussions between supporters of rival paradigms should be persuasion rather than compulsion. I suggest that what I have summarized in this paragraph is what lies behind Kuhn's claim that rival paradigms are "incommensurable".

A scientific revolution corresponds to the abandonment of one paradigm and the adoption of a new one, not by an individual scientist only but by the relevant scientific community as a whole. As more and more individual scientists, for a variety of reasons, are converted to the new paradigm there is an "increasing shift in the distribution of professional allegiances".[9] If the revolution is to be successful, then this shift will spread so as to include the majority of the relevant scientific community, leaving only a few dissenters. These will be excluded from the new scientific community and will perhaps takes refuge in a philosophy department. In any case, they will eventually die.

4. The function of normal science and revolutions

Some aspects of Kuhn's writings might give the impression that his account of the nature of science is a purely *descriptive* one, that is, that he aims to do nothing more than to describe scientific theories or paradigms and the activity of scientists. Were this the case, then Kuhn's account of science would be of little value as a *theory* of science. A putative theory of science based only on description would be open to some of the same objections as were levelled against the naive inductivist account of how scientific theories themselves are arrived at. Unless the descriptive account of science is shaped by some theory, no guidance is offered as to what kinds of activities and products of activities are to be described. In particular, the activities and productions of hack scientists would need to be documented in as much detail as the achievements of an Einstein or a Galileo.

However, it is a mistake to regard Kuhn's characterization of science as arising solely from a description of the work of scientists. Kuhn insists that his account constitutes a theory of science because it includes an explanation of the *function* of its various components. According to Kuhn, normal science and revolutions serve necessary functions, so that science must either involve those characteristics or some others that would serve to perform the same functions. Let us see what those functions are, according to Kuhn.

Periods of normal science provide the opportunity for scientists to develop the esoteric details of a theory. Working within a paradigm, the fundamentals of which they take for granted, they are able to perform the exacting experimental and theoretical work necessary to improve the match between the paradigm and nature to an ever-greater degree. It is through their confidence in the adequacy of a paradigm that scientists are able to devote their energies to attempts to solve the detailed puzzles presented to them within the paradigm, rather than engage in disputes about the legitimacy of their fundamental assumptions and methods. It is necessary for normal science to be to a large extent uncritical. If all scientists were critical of all parts of the framework in which they worked all of the time then no detailed work would ever get done.

If all scientists were and remained normal scientists then a particular science would become trapped in a single paradigm and would never progress beyond it. This would be a serious fault, from the Kuhnian point of view. A paradigm embodies a particular conceptual framework through which the world is viewed and in which it is described, and a particular set of experimental and theoretical techniques for matching the paradigm with nature. But there is no *a priori* reason to expect that any one paradigm is perfect or even the best available. There are no inductive procedures for arriving at perfectly adequate paradigms. Consequently, science should contain within it a means of breaking out of one paradigm into a better one. This is the function of revolutions. All paradigms will be inadequate to some extent as far as their match with nature is concerned. When the mismatch becomes serious, that is, when a crisis develops, the revolutionary step of replacing the entire paradigm by another becomes essential for the effective progress of science.

Progress through revolutions is Kuhn's alternative to the cumulative progress characteristic of inductivist accounts of science. According to the latter view, scientific knowledge grows continuously as more numerous and more various observations are made, enabling new concepts to be formed, old ones to be refined, and new lawful relationships between them to be discovered. From Kuhn's particular point of view, this is mistaken because it ignores the role played by paradigms in guiding observation and experiment. It is just because paradigms have such a persuasive influence on the science practised within them that the replacement of one by another must be a revolutionary one.

One other function catered for in Kuhn's account is worth mentioning. Kuhn's paradigms are not so precise that they can be replaced by an explicit set of rules, as was mentioned above. Different scientists or groups of scientists may well interpret and apply the paradigm in a somewhat different way. Faced with the same situation, not all scientists will reach the same decision or adopt the same strategy. This has the advantage that the number of strategies attempted will be multiplied. Risks are thus distributed through the scientific community, and the chances of some long-term success are increased. "How else", asks Kuhn, "could the group as a whole hedge its bets?"[10]

FURTHER READING

Kuhn's major work is, of course, *The Structure of Scientific Revolutions.* The 1970 edition of the book (Chicago: Chicago University Press) contains a *Postscript* in which his views are refined and modified to some extent. Kuhn's modification of his original idea of a paradigm is discussed in more detail in "Second Thoughts on Paradigms", in *The Structure of Scientific*

Theories, ed. F. Suppe (Urbana: University of Illinois Press, 1973), pp.459-82. Criticism and the Growth of Knowledge, ed. I. Lakatos and A. Musgrave (Cambridge: Cambridge University Press, 1974), contains papers involving a clash between the Popperian and Kuhnian approaches to science. Kuhn compares his views with Popper's in "Logic of Discovery or Psychology of Research?", pp.1-23, and replies to his Popperian critics in "Reflections on My Critics", pp.231-78. A more recent collection of essays by Kuhn is *The Essential Tension: Selected Studies in Scientific Tradition and Change* (Chicago: Chicago University Press, 1977). The extent to which Kuhn's position is primarily a sociological one is very evident in his "Comment [on the Relation between Science and Art]", *Comparative Studies in Society and History* 11 (1969): 403-12. D. Bloor defends Kuhn against Lakatos in "Two Paradigms of Scientific Knowledge?", *Science Studies* 1 (1971): 101-15. For an attempt to axiomatize Kuhn's view of science (!) by J. Sneed, and a discussion of that attempt by Kuhn and W. Stegmuller, see Proceedings of the 5th International Congress of Logic, Methodology and Philosophy of Science in London, Ontario, August-September 1975.

1. T.S. Kuhn, *The Structure of Scientific Revolutions* (Chicago: University of Chicago Press, 1970).
2. Since first writing *The Structure of Scientific Revolutions,* Kuhn has conceded that he originally used "paradigm" in an ambiguous sense. In the *Postscript* to the 1970 edition, he distinguishes a general sense of the term, which he now refers to as the *"disciplinary matrix",* and a narrow sense of the term, which he has replaced by *"exemplar".* I continue to use "paradigm" in its general sense, to refer to what Kuhn has renamed the disciplinary matrix.
3. Cf. Lakatos's somewhat more precise notion of a positive heuristic.
4. See M. Polanyi, *Personal Knowledge* (London: Routledge and Kegan Paul, 1973) and *Knowing and Being* (London: Routledge and Kegan Paul, 1969).
5. Kuhn, *The Structure of Scientific Revolutions,* pp.67-68.
6. Ibid., p.84.
7. Ibid., p.91.
8. Ibid., pp.93-94.
9. Ibid., p.158.
10. I. Lakatos and A. Musgrave, eds., (Cambridge: Cambridge University Press, 1974) *Criticism and the Growth of Knowledge,* p.241.

9

Rationalism versus Relativism

In the previous two chapters I have summarized two contemporary analyses of science that differ in fundamental respects. Lakatos and Kuhn offer conflicting distinctions between science and non-science or pseudo-science. The clash between Kuhn's views, on the one hand, and those of Lakatos, and also Popper, on the other, has given rise to a debate concerning two contrasting positions associated with the terms "rationalism" and "relativisim" respectively. The debate is over the issues of theory appraisal and theory choice and over ways of demarcating science from non-science. In this chapter, I will first characterize two positions that represent the extremes of the debate, extremes that I will refer to as rationalism and relativism respectively. Then I will proceed to discuss the extent to which Lakatos and Kuhn can legitimately be characterized as rationalists or relativists.

In the final section, I will begin to cast some doubt on the terms in which the debate has been set.

1. Rationalism

The extreme rationalist asserts that there is a single, timeless, universal criterion with reference to which the relative merits of rival theories are to be assessed. For example, an inductivist might take as his universal criterion the degree of inductive support a theory receives from accepted facts, whilst a falsificationist might base his criterion on the degree of falsifiability of unfalsified theories. Whatever the details of a rationalist's formulation of the criterion, an important feature of it is its universality and ahistorical character. The universal criterion will be invoked when judging the relative merits of the physics of Aristotle and Democritus, Ptolemaic and Copernican astronomy, Freudian and behaviourist psychology or the big bang and steady state theories of the universe. The extreme rationalist sees the decisions and choices of scientists as being guided by the universal criterion. The rational scientist will reject theories that fail to live up to it and, when choosing between two rival theories, will choose the one that lives up to it best. The typical rationalist will believe that theories that meet the demands of the universal criterion are true or approximately true or probably true.[1] The quotation on page 10 describes how a scientist, who is "superhuman" insofar as he always acts rationally, would operate according to an inductivist rationalist.

The distinction between science and non-science is straightforward for the rationalist. Only those theories that are such that they can be clearly assessed in terms of the universal criterion and which survive the test are scientific. Thus an inductivist rationalist might rule that astrology is not a science because it is not inductively derivable from the facts of observation, whilst a falsificationist might rule that Marxism is not scientific because it is not falsifiable. The typical rationalist will take it as self-evident that a high value is to be placed on knowledge developed in accordance with the universal criterion. This will be especially so if the process is understood as leading towards truth. Truth, rationality, and hence science, are seen as intrinsically good.

2. Relativism

The relativist denies that there is a universal, ahistorical standard of rationality with respect to which one theory can be judged better than another. What counts as better or worse with respect to scientific theories will vary from individual to individual or from community to community. The aim of knowledge-seeking will depend on what is important for or what is valued by the individual or community in question. For example, a high status will typically be attributed to the aim of acquiring material control over nature within Western capitalist societies, but will be accredited with a low status in a culture in which knowledge is designed to produce feelings of contentment or peace.

The dictum of the ancient Greek philosopher Protagoras, "man is the measure of all things", expresses a relativism with respect to individuals, whilst Kuhn's remark "there is no standard higher than the assent of the relevant community" expresses a relativism with respect to communities.[2] Characterizations of progress and specifications of criteria for judging the merits of theories will always be relative to the individual or community that subscribes to them.

Decisions and choices made by scientists or groups of scientists will be governed by what is valued by those individuals or groups. In a given choice situation, there is no universal criterion that dictates a decision that is logically compelling for the "rationa'l" scientist. An understanding of the choices made by a particular scientist will require an understanding of what that scientist values and will involve psychological investigation, whilst the choices made by a community will depend on what it values and an understanding of those choices will involve sociological investigation. Boris Hessen's account of the adoption of Newtonian physics in the seventeenth century as a response to the technological needs of the time can be read as a relativist account with respect to communities, whilst Feyerabend's assertion that it is the "internal connectedness of all the parts of the (Copernican) system together with his belief in the basic nature of circular motion that makes Copernicus pronounce the motion of the earth as real" is a remark in keeping with a relativism with respect to individuals.[3]

Since, for the relativist, the criteria for judging the merits of theories will depend on the values or interests of the individual or community entertaining them, the distinction between science and non-science will vary accordingly. Thus, a theory of the tides based on the moon's attraction was good science for Newtonians but bordered on occult mysticism for Galileo, whilst in contemporary society, Marx's theory of historical change is good science for some and propaganda for others. For the extreme relativist, the distinction between science and non-science becomes much more arbitrary and less important that it is for the rationalist. A relativist will deny that there is a unique category, "science", that is intrinsically superior to other forms of knowledge, although it may well be that individuals or communities place a high value on what is usually referred to as science. If "science" (the relativist might well be inclined to use quotation marks) is highly regarded in our society, then this is to be understood by analyzing our society, and not simply by analyzing the nature of science.

With these caricatures of rationalism and relativism as a reference point, let us now consider where Lakatos and Kuhn fit into the picture.

3. Lakatos as rationalist

Some of Lakatos's writings indicate that he wished to defend a position something like the one I have labelled rationalism, and that he viewed with horror the position I have labelled relativism, a version of which he attributed to Kuhn. According to Lakatos, the debate "concerns our central intellectual values".[4] Lakatos explicitly stated that the "central problem in philosophy of science is . . . the problem of stating *universal* conditions under which a theory is scientific", a problem which is "closely linked with the problem of the rationality of science" and whose solution "ought to give us guidance as to when the acceptance of a scientific theory is rational or not".[5] In Lakatos's view, a relativist position according to which there is no standard higher than that of the relevant community leaves us with no way of criticizing that standard. If there is "no way of judging a theory but by assessing the number, faith and vocal energy of its supporters", then truth lies in power",[6] scientific change becomes a matter of "mob psychology" and scientific progress is essentially a "bandwagon effect".[7] In the absence of rational criteria to guide theory choice, theory change becomes akin to religious conversion.[8]

Lakatos's rhetoric, then, does not leave room for much doubt that he wished to defend a rationalist position and deplored the relativist position. Let us make a careful assessment of the extent to which he succeeded in defending a rationalist position.

Lakatos's universal criterion for the assessment of theories follows from his principle "the methodology of scientific research programmes is better suited for approximating the truth in our actual universe than any other methodology".[9] Science progresses by way of competiton between research programmes. A research programme is better than a rival if it is more progressive, the progressive nature of a programme depending on its degree of coherence and the extent to which it has led to successful novel predictions, as discussed in Chapter 7. The aim of science is truth, and, according to Lakatos, the methodology of research programmes provides the best means of assessing the extent to which we have succeeded in approaching it.

"I [Lakatos] give criteria of progression and stagnation within a programme and also rules for the 'elimination' of whole research programmes".[10] By defining standards of rationality "the methodology of research programmes might help us in devising laws for stemming . . . intellectual pollution".[11] Remarks such as these indicate that Lakatos aimed to propose a universal criterion for judging research programmes in particular and scientific progress in general.

Whilst Lakatos did propose what was intended to be a universal criterion of rationality or scientificity, he did not regard this criterion as a consequence of logic alone, or somehow God-given. He regarded it as a testable conjecture. The adequacy of the conjecture is to be tested by confronting it with the history of science, or, more precisely, given the historical work done by Lakatos and his followers, by confronting it with the history of physics.[12] Roughly speaking, a proposed methodology (and its associated characterization of what constitutes progress) is to be evaluated by the extent to which it is able to account for "good" science and its history. At first glance, this mode of proceeding appears circular. The methodology determines those theories from the history of physics that constitutes good physics whilst it is just those good theories against which the methodology is to be tested. However, given the details of Lakatos's account and Worrall's clarification of it, this is not so. There are genuine ways in which tests against the history of physics can support or discredit Lakatos's methodology. Lakatos's theory gains support if it can be shown that episodes in the history of science, that have been inexplicable in terms of rival methodologies, are explicable in terms of the methodology of research programmes. For example, Worrall's study of the rejection of Thomas Young's wave theory of light and the retention of Newton's corpuscular theory in the early nineteenth century supports Lakatos. The rejection of Young's theory, which poses problems from the point of view of rival methodologies and which had been explained by easily discredited theories such as an appeal to hero worship of Newton, is shown by Worrall to be in complete accord with Lakatos's methodology. A second way in which Lakatos's methodology could conceivably be supported is as follows: The methodology might serve to identify a programme that received strong support from the scientific community but which does not conform to the methodology of research programmes, and this identification might subsequently lead to the novel discovery of some external cause, such as the intervention of some government or industrial monopoly. If an episode in the history of science does not conform to Lakatos's methodology, and if no satisfactory, independently supported, external explanation can be found, this would constitute evidence against the methodology, especially if a rival methodology can cope with the historical example in a superior way.

Lakatos offers a universal criterion of rationality, then, which is conjectural and is to be tested against the history of science. Further, the claim is made that his criterion has withstood tests against episodes from the last two hundred or so years of physics in a superior way to rival criteria that have been proposed. The historical case studies carried out by Lakatos and his followers certainly lend some support to that latter claim.

Some of Lakatos's remarks suggest that his criterion of rationality was intended to guide theory choice. This is suggested by the quotations earlier in the section, which indicate that Lakatos hoped to give rules for eliminating research programmes and stemming intellectual pollution. However, in spite of remarks like these, Lakatos's methodology is not capable of yielding advice for scientists, and Lakatos acknowledged this.[13] In particular, it is not a consequence of Lakatos's methodology that scientists should adopt progressive programmes and abandon degenerating ones. It is always possible that a degenerating programme might make a come-back. "One can be 'wise' only after the event . . . One *must* realise that one's opponent, even if lagging badly behind, may still stage a come-back. No advantage for one side can ever be regarded as absolutely conclusive."[14] Consequently, "one may rationally stick to a degenerating programme until it is overtaken by a rival *and even after*".[15] Although Lakatos's methodology embodies a definition of what progress in modern physics has consisted in, it does not offer guidance to those who aim to achieve such progress. His methodology "is more of a guide to the historian of science than the scientist".[16] Lakatos failed to offer the rationalist account of science that many of his remarks indicate he intended to give.

According to Lakatos, a field of enquiry is a science if it conforms to the methodology of scientific research programmes and is not if it does not, bearing in mind that this is a conjecture to be tested against the history of physics. It is evident that Lakatos took it for granted that physics constitutes the paradigm of rationality and good science. He assumed, without argument, that science, as exemplified by physics, is superior to forms of knowledge that do not share its methodological characteristics. At one place he described the statement "physics has higher verisimilitude than astrology" as plausible and asks why it should not be accepted as long as no serious alternative is offered.[17] This highlights a serious weakness in his philosophy. Lakatos presented his methodology as a response to the problem of distinguishing rationality from irrationality, of stemming intellectual pollution and of throwing light on questions "of vital social and political relevance" such as the status of Marxism or contemporary research in genetics.[18] It would appear that a large part of the answer was assumed by him from the outset and without argument. Lakatos assumed that any field of enquiry that does not share the main characteristics of physics is not science and is inferior to it from the point of view of rationality.[19]

4. Kuhn as relativist

Kuhn mentions a number of criteria that can be used in assessing whether one theory is better than a rival. They include "accuracy of prediction, particularly of quantitative prediction; the balance between esoteric and everyday subject matter; and the number of different problems solved" and also, although less importantly, "simplicity, scope and compatibility with other specialities".[20] Criteria such as these constitute the values of the scientific community. The means by which these values are specified "must, in the final analysis, be psychological or sociological. It must, that is, be a description of a value system, an ideology, together with an analysis of the institutions through which that system is transmitted and enforced".[21] "There is no standard higher than the assent of the relevant community."[22] These aspects of Kuhn's position conform to my characterization of relativism. Whether or not one theory is better than another is to be judged relative to the standards of the appropriate community, and those standards will typically vary with the cultural and historical setting of the community. Kuhn's relativism is emphasized in the concluding sentences of the postscript to *The Structure of Scientific Revolutions*. "Scientific knowledge, like language, is intrinsically the common property of a group or else nothing at all. To understand it we shall need to know the special characteristics of the groups that create and use it."[23]

Kuhn denies that he is a relativist. Responding to the charge that he is one, he wrote: "Later scientific theories are better than earlier ones for solving puzzles in the often quite different environments to which they are applied. That is not a relativist's position, and it displays the sense in which I am a convinced believer in scientific progress."[24] From this it would seem that Kuhn is a rationalist specifying a universal criterion with respect to which the relative merits of theories can be assessed, namely, problem-solving ability. I do not think that Kuhn's claim that his position is not relativist can be sustained. He himself remarks that considerations based on problem-solving ability are "neither individually nor collectively compelling" as far as the relative merits of competing paradigms are concerned, and that "aesthetic considerations (according to which the new theory is said to be 'neater', 'more suitable' or 'simpler' than the old) can sometimes be decisive".[25] This brings us back to a relativist position. A further problem with a universal criterion for progress based on problem-solving ability is the difficulty of specifying that notion in a non-relativist way. Kuhn's own account of science entails that what is to count as a problem is paradigm or community dependent. My own favourite example concerns the determination of the atomic and molecular weights of naturally occuring elements and compounds in the nineteenth century. These accurate determinations constituted important problems at the time. From the twentieth century point of view it can be appreciated that naturally occuring compounds contain what, from the point of view of theoretical chemistry, is an arbitrary and theoretically uninteresting mixture of isotopes so that, as F. Soddy remarked, the painstaking endeavour of the nineteenth century chemists "appears as of as little interest and significance as the determination of the average weight of a collection of bottles, some of them full and some of them more or less empty".[26]

Whist Kuhn maintains that science does progress in some sense, he is quite unambiguous in his denial that it can be said to progress towards the truth in any well-defined sense. In Chapter 13 I will try to explain why I agree with him on this point.

On the question of theory choice, Kuhn insists that there are no criteria of choice that are logically compelling. "There is no neutral algorithm for theory choice, no systematic decision procedure which, properly applied, must lead each individual in the group to the same decision."[27] Within a scientific community there will exist community sanctioned values guiding the choices of individual scientists, including accuracy, scope, simplicity, fruitfulness and the like. Scientists holding these values may make different choices in the same concrete situation. This is due to the fact that they may attribute different weight to the various values, and also may apply the same criterion differently in the same concrete situation.

For Kuhn, whether a field qualifies as a science or not depends on whether or not it conforms to the account of science offered in *The Structure of Scientific Revolutions*. The most important feature of a field of enquiry with respect to the distinction between science and non-science, Kuhn claims, is the extent to which that field is able to support a normal science tradition. In Kuhn's words "it is hard to find another criterion that so clearly proclaims a field a science".[28]

Kuhn's demarcation criterion has been criticized by Popper on the grounds that it gives undue emphasis to the role of criticism in science; by Lakatos because, among other things, it misses the importance of competition between research programmes (or paradigms); and by Feyerabend on the grounds that Kuhn's distinction leads to the conclusion that organized crime and Oxford philosophy qualify as science.[29]

Like Lakatos, Kuhn does not argue that science is superior to other fields of enquiry, but assumes it. Indeed, he suggests that if a theory of rationality should clash with science then we should change our theory of rationality. "To suppose, instead, that we possess criteria of rationality which are independent of our understanding of the essentials of the scientific progress is to open the door to cloud-cuckoo land."[30] This unquestioned high regard for science, as the exemplar of rationality, which Kuhn shares with Lakatos, is, I suggest, the one respect in which Kuhn's position differs from relativism as I have characterized it.

Lakatos's use of terms such as contagious panic with reference to Kuhn's characterization of crisis states and "mob psychology" in reference to his characterization of revolutions is too extreme. However, there is an element of truth in them. In Kuhn's account of science the values operative in the process of science and determining the acceptance and rejection of theories are to be discerned by psychological and sociological analysis of the scientific community. When this is taken in conjunction with the assumption that contemporary science is the epitome of rationality at its best, we are left with a conservative position. Kuhn's position leaves us with no way of criticizing the decisions and mode of operating of the scientific community. Whilst sociological analysis is basic within Kuhn's account, he offers very little in the way of sociological theory and offers no suggestions of how acceptable and unacceptable ways of reaching a consensus are to be distinguished. Lakatos's account fares slightly better in this respect insofar as it does offer means by which *some* decisions of the scientific community might be criticized.

The discussion of this chapter so far might perhaps be summed up by noting that Lakatos aimed to give a rationalist account of science but failed, whilst Kuhn denied that he aimed to give a relativist account of science but gave one nevertheless.

5. Towards changing the terms of the debate

In this chapter the discussion of rationalism and relativism has been concerned almost exclusively with appraisals and judgements about aspects of knowledge. We have considered various analyses of the kind of criteria that enable individuals or groups to judge whether one theory is better than a rival, or whether or not a particular body of knowledge is scientific. The appropriateness of that kind of question for understanding the nature of science in a fundamental way is brought into question when it is pointed out that there is what would seem to be a fairly straightforward distinction between some state of affairs and judgements about that state of affairs made by individuals or groups. Is it not possible, for example, that some theory is better, in the sense of being closer to the truth, a better problem solver, a better instrument of prediction or whatever, than a rival, even though no individual or group judges it to be so? Is it not the case that individuals or groups can be wrong in their judgements about the nature or status of some theory? The posing of this kind of question suggests that there might well be a way of analyzing science, its aims and its mode of progress, that focuses on features of science itself, irrespective of what individuals or groups might think. In the following chapter I will prepare the way for an analysis of that kind and in Chapter 11 I will propose an account of theory change in physics that does not hinge on the judgements of individuals or groups.

FURTHER READING

The classic source for the debate between Kuhn on the one hand and Popper and Lakatos on the other is I. Lakatos and A. Musgrave, *Criticism and the Growth of Knowledge* (Cambridge: Cambridge University Press, 1979). A sequel to this volume is G. Radnitzky and G. Anderson, *Progress and Rationality in Science* (Dordrecht: Reidel Publishing Co., 1978). Lakatos's position is discussed and criticized in R.S. Cohen, P.K. Feyerabend and M.W. Wartofsky, *Essays in Memory of Imre Lakatos* (Dordrecht: Reidel Publishing Co., 1976). Of particular interest is Alan Musgrave's article "Method or Madness?" on pp.457-91. Lakatos's defence of rationality is criticized by Feyerabend in *Against Method* (London: New Left Books, 1975), Ch. 16., and in his "On the Critique of Scientific *Reason*", in C. Howson, ed., *Method and Appraisal in the Physical*

Sciences (Cambridge: Cambridge University Press, 1976), pp.309-39. A very clear and readable account of a relativist position similar to Kuhn's is Harold I. Brown, *Perception, Theory and Commitment: The New Philosophy of Science* (Chicago: University of Chiago Press, 1977). A relativist account of science in the sociology of knowledge tradition is D. Bloor, *Knowledge and Social Imagery* (London: Routledge and Kegan Paul, 1976). A useful attempt to clarify some of the issues in the debate between rationalism and relativism is Denise Russell, "Scepticism in Recent Epistemology", *Methodology and Science* 14 (1981): 139-54.

1. The notion of truth is problematic. It will be discussed in some detail in chapter 13.
2. Kuhn's remark is on p.94 of *The Structure of Scientific Revolutions*. Whether it adequately expresses his overall view will be discussed in section 4.
3. Hessen's account, "The Social and Economic Roots of Newton's 'Principia' ", is in N.I. Bukharin et al., *Science at the Crossroads* (London: Cass, 1971), pp.149-212. The Feyerabend quotation is from his *Science in a Free Society* (London: New Left Books, 1978), p.50.
4. I. Lakatos and A. Musgrave, eds., *Criticism and the Growth of Knowledge* (Cambridge: Cambridge University Press, 1974), p.93.
5. J. Worrall and G. Currie, eds., *Imre Lakatos. Philosophical Papers. Volume I: The Methodology of Scientific Research Programmes* (Cambridge: Cambridge University Press, 1978), pp.168-69, italics in original.
6. Lakatos and Musgrave (1974), p.93.
7. Ibid., p.178.
8. Ibid., p.93.
9. Worrall and Currie (1978), vol. 1, p.165, n2.
10. Ibid., p.112.
11. Lakatos and Musgrave (1974), p.176.
12. The details of the way in which Lakatos conceived of his methodology being tested against the history of physics are presented in his essay "History of Science and its Rational Reconstructions", reprinted in Worrall and Currie (1978), vol. 1, pp.102-38. It has been clarified and improved by John Worrall in section 5 of his "Thomas Young and the 'refutation' of Newtonian optics: a case study of the interaction of philosophy of science and history of science", in C. Howson, ed., *Method and Appraisal in the Physical Sciences* (Cambridge: Cambridge University Press, 1976), pp.107-79.
13. "I, of course, do not prescribe to the individual scientist what to try to do in a situation characterised by two rival progressive research programmes . . . Whatever they *have* done, I can judge: I can say whether they have made progress or not. But I cannot advise them — and do not wish to advise them — about exactly what to worry about and in which direction they should seek progress." I. Lakatos, "Replies to Critics", in *Boston Studies in the Philosophy of Science,* vol. 8, ed., R. Buck and R.S. Cohen (Dordrecht: Reidel Publishing Co., 1971), p.178, italics in original.
14. Worrall and Currie (1978), vol. 1, p.113, italics in original.
15. Ibid., p.117, italics in original.
16. Ibid., p.154.

17. Ibid., p.166.
18. See, for example, his essay "Science and Pseudo-Science" in Worrall and Currie (1978), vol. 1, pp.1-7.
19. Feyerabend in "On the Critique of Scientific Reason" in Howson (1976), pp.309-39 distinguishes between the questions "What is science?" and "What's so great about science?" and observes that Lakatos offered nothing by way of an answer to the second.
20. *The Structure of Scientific Revolutions,* p.154.
21. Lakatos and Musgrave (1974), p. 21.
22. *The Structure of Scientific Revolutions,* p.94.
23. Ibid., p.210.
24. Ibid., p.206.
25. Ibid., p.206.
26. As quoted by Lakatos in Lakatos and Musgrave (1974), p.140.
27. *The Structure of Scientific Revolutions,* p.200.
28. Ibid., p.22.
29. Popper's criticism is in his "Normal Science and its Dangers", in Lakatos and Musgrave (1974), 51-58; Lakatos's is in ibid., p.155; and Feyerabend's in ibid., 200-201.
30. Lakatos and Musgrave (1974), p.264.

10

Objectivism

In the way I will use the term, objectivism with respect to human knowledge is a view which stresses that items of knowledge, from simple propositions to complex theories, have properties and characteristics that transcend the beliefs and states of awareness of the individuals that devise and contemplate them. (It would be in keeping with the objectivist standpoint to observe that the very view of objectivism I am presenting in this chapter may possess contradictions or may lead to consequences of which I am not aware and which I would not welcome.) Objectivism is opposed to a view that I will refer to as individualism, according to which knowledge is understood in terms of beliefs held by individuals. In order to clarify what objectivism involves it will be helpful to say a little about individualism first and then contrast objectivism with it.

1. Individualism

From the individualist point of view knowledge is understood to be a special set of beliefs held by individuals and residing in their minds or brains. That view certainly gains support from common usage. If I say, "I know the date on which I wrote this particular paragraph, but you do not", then I am referring to something that is among my beliefs, and in a sense resides in my mind or brain, but is not among your beliefs and is absent from your mind or brain. If I ask the question, "Do you or do you not know Newton's first law of motion?", I am asking a question about what you, as an individual, are acquainted with. It is clear that the individualist who accepts this way of understanding knowledge in terms of belief will not accept all beliefs as constituting genuine knowledge. If I believe that Newton's first law reads, "Apples fall downwards", then I am simply mistaken and my mistaken belief will not constitute knowledge. If a belief is to count as genuine knowledge, then it must be possible to justify the belief by showing it to be true, or perhaps probably true, by appeal to appropriate evidence. "Knowledge, on this view, is true belief properly evidenced, or some similar formula."[1]

If knowledge is viewed from the individualist point of view it is not difficult to see how a fundamental problem arises. It is the so-called infinite regress of reasons that dates back at least as far as Plato. If some statement is to be justified, then this will be done by appeal to other statements which constitute the evidence for it. But this gives rise to the problem of how the statements constituting the evidence are themselves to be justified. If we justify them by further appeal to more evidential statements then the problem repeats itself and will continue to repeat itself unless a way can be found to halt the infinite regress that threatens. To take a straightforward example, suppose I am faced with the problem of justifying Kepler's first law, that planets move in ellipses around the sun. If I do this by showing that its approximate validity follows from Newton's laws my justification is incomplete unless I can justify Newton's laws. If I attempt to justify Newton's laws by appeal to experimental evidence then the question of the validity of the experimental evidence arises, and so on. If the problem of the infinite regress is to be avoided, it would seem that what is needed is some set of statements that do not need to be justified by appeal to other statements but are in some sense self-justifying. Such a set of statements would then constitute the *foundations of knowledge,* and any beliefs that are to acquire the status of knowledge would need to be justified by tracing them back to the foundations.

If the problem of knowledge is construed in this way, it is not difficult to see how two rival traditions in the theory of knowledge, classical rationalism[2] and empiricism, arise. Speaking very roughly and sweepingly, we can argue as follows. Individual human beings have two ways of acquiring knowledge about the world, thinking and observing. If we give priority to the first mode over the second we arrive at a classical rationalist theory of knowledge, whilst if we give priority to the second over the first we arrive at an empiricist theory.

According to the classical rationalist, true foundations of knowledge are accessible to the thinking mind. The propositions that constitute those foundations are revealed as clear, distinct and self-evidently true by careful reasoning and comtemplation. The classic illustration of the rationalist conception of knowledge is Euclidean geometry. The foundations of that particular body of knowledge are conceived to be the axioms, statements such as "only one straight line can be drawn joining two points". It can plausibly be said of such axioms that they are self-evidently true (although from a modern point of view some of them are false in the light of Einstein's theory of general relativity). Once they are established as true then all of the theorems that follow deductively from them will also be true. The self-evident axioms constitute the secure foundations with respect to which geometrical knowledge is justified, according to the rationalist ideal. The first modern classical rationalist of the kind I have sketched here was Rene Descartes.

For a classical empiricist, true foundations of knowledge are accessible to individuals by way of the senses. It is presumed by empiricists that individuals can establish some statements as true by confronting the world through their senses. The statements so established constitute the foundations on which further knowledge is to be built by some kind of inductive inference. John Locke was one of the early modern empiricists. The inductivist view of science sketched in Chapter 1 of this book represents a brand of empiricism.

2. Objectivism

An individual born into this world is born into a world in which there already exists much knowledge. Someone who aims to become a physicist will be confronted with a body of knowledge that represents the current state of development of physics, much of which he will need to become acquainted with if he is to make a contribution to the field. The objectivist gives priority, in his analysis of knowledge, to the characteristics of items or bodies of knowledge that individuals are confronted with, independently of the attitudes, beliefs or other subjective states of those individuals. Loosely speaking, knowledge is treated as something outside rather than inside the minds or brains of individuals.

The objectivist emphasis can be illustrated by reference to very simple propositions. Given a language, propositions within it will have properties whether individuals are aware of them or not or believe it or not. For instance, the proposition, "my cat and I live in a house that no animals inhabit," has the property of being contradictory, whilst the propositions "I have a cat" and "today a guinea pig died" have the property of being consequences of the proposition "today my white cat killed someone's pet guinea pig". In these simple examples, the fact that the propositions have the properties I have singled out will be fairly obvious to anyone who contemplates them, but this need not be so. For example, a lawyer in a murder trial may, after much painstaking analysis, discover the fact that one witness's report contradicts that of another. If this is indeed the case, then it is the case whatever the witnesses intended and whether or not they were aware of it or believed it. What is more, if the lawyer in our example had not discovered the inconsistency it may have remained undiscovered so that no-one ever became aware of it. Nevertheless, the fact would remain that the two witnesses' reports were inconsistent. Propositions, then, can have properties quite independently of what any individual might be aware of. They have "objective" properties.

The maze of propositions involved in a body of knowledge at some stage in its development will, in a similar way, have properties that individuals working on it need not be aware of. The theoretical structure that is modern physics is so complex that it clearly cannot be identified with the beliefs of any one physicist or group of physicists. Many scientists contribute in their separate ways with their separate skills to the growth and articulation of physics, just as many workers combine their efforts in the construction of a cathedral. And just as a happy steeplejack may be blissfully unaware of the implication of some ominous discovery made by labourers digging near the cathedral's foundations, so a lofty theoretician may be unaware of the relevance of some new experimental finding for the theory on which he works. In either case, relationships may objectively exist between parts of the structure independently of any individual's awareness of that relationship.

A strong point in favour of the objectivist position is that scientific theories can and often do have consequences that were unintended by the original proponents of the theory and of which those proponents were unaware. These consequences, such as the prediction of a novel kind of phenomenon or an unexpected clash with some other area of theory, exist as properties of the new theory that are there to be discovered by further scientific practice. Thus Poisson was able to discover and demonstrate that Fresnel's wave theory of light had the consequence that there should be a bright spot at the centre of the shadow side of an illuminated disc, a consequence of which Fresnel himself had been unaware. Various clashes between Fresnel's theory and the Newtonian particle theory, which it challenged, were also discovered. For example, the former predicted that light should travel faster in air than in water, while the latter predicted that the speed in water should be the greater. Episodes such as these provide persuasive evidence for the view that scientific theories have an objective structure outside of the minds of individual scientists and have properties that may or may not be discovered or produced and may or may not be properly understood by individual scientists or groups of scientists. Here is a slightly more detailed example, which should serve to emphasize the point and will also lead on to another related one.

When Clerk Maxwell developed his electromagnetic theory in the 1860s, he had a number of explicit aims in mind. One of these was to develop a mechanical explanation of electromagnetic phenomena. Maxwell wished to put Faraday's theory, involving concepts such as "lines of force" etc., on what he saw as surer foundations by reducing it to a mechanical theory of a mechanical aether. In the course of his efforts, Maxwell found it convenient to introduce a new concept, his displacement current. One of the attractive consequences of this move was that it led to the possibility of an electromagnetic explanation of the nature of light, as Maxwell was able to show. The points I wish to stress in the present context are these. Firstly, Maxwell was and remained unaware of one of the most dramatic consequences of his own theory, namely, that it predicted a new kind of phenomenon, radio waves, which can be generated by oscillating electrical sources.[3] That Maxwell's theory did in fact have this consequence, in spite of the fact that Maxwell did not realize it, was discovered and clearly demonstrated, after a few false starts, by G.F. Fitzgerald in 1881, two years after Maxwell's death. The second point is that the formulation of electromagnetic theory by Maxwell was to mark the first step towards the undermining of the view that the whole of the physical world is to be explained as a material system governed by Newton's laws, a view that Maxwell and his school avidly supported. The objective relationship between Newton's theory and Maxwell's theory is such that the latter cannot be reduced to the former, although this was not appreciated until the early decades of the twentieth century. The programme of reducing electromagnetism to the mechanics of an aether, the desirability of which commanded a consensus in the Maxwellian school, was a programme that was doomed from the very outset.

More can be said of this example, which lends support to the claim that problem situations have an objective existence. While Maxwellians such as Oliver Lodge and Joseph Larmor were attempting to devise aether models, some physicists on the Continent had discerned another programme stemming from Maxwell's theory. H.A. Lorentz in Holland and H. Hertz in Germany came to learn that Maxwell's theory could be fruitfully extended and applied to new situations by ignoring the mechanical aether allegedly underlying the field quantities and by concentrating on and investigating the properties of the fields as interrelated by Maxwell's equations. This path proved very fruitful and was eventually to lead to Einstein's special theory of relativity. The point to be stressed here is that the programme that Lorentz, Hertz and others actually pursued was already present in the writings of Maxwell in the form of an objectively existing opportunity, an opportunity that the Maxwellians did not fully grasp but which Lorentz did.

Popper has drawn an analogy between objectively existing problem situations within science and a nesting-box in his garden. The nesting box represents an objectively existing problem situation and opportunity for birds. One day, some birds may grasp the opportunity, solve the problem and successfully utilize the box to build a nest. The problem and opportunity exist for birds whether they respond to them or not. In an analagous way, problem situations exist within the theoretical structure of science whether or not they are appreciated and taken advantage of by scientists. The fact that problem situations provide objective opportunities helps to explain the examples of simultaneous discoveries in science, such as the simultaneous "discovery" of the law of conservation of energy by several independent workers in the 1840s. When pursuing questions concerning the status of some theory or research programme, then, objectivists will focus attention on the features of those theories or programmes rather than on the beliefs, feelings of conviction or other attitudes of the individuals or groups that work on them. They will be concerned, for example, with the relationship between Newton's theory and Galileo's theory, and will be particularly interested to show in what sense the former can be said to be an advance on the latter. They will not be concerned with questions about the attitudes of Galileo or Newton to their theories. Whether or not Galileo firmly believed in the truth of his theories will not be of fundamental importance for an understanding of physics and its growth, although it would, of course, be important if the aim were to understand Galileo.

3. Science as a social practice

So far I have outlined an objectivist view that focuses on theories as explicitly expressed in verbal or mathematical propositions. However, there is more to science than this. There is also the practical aspect of a science. A science, at some stage in its development, will involve a set of techniques for articulating, applying and testing the theories of which it is comprised. The development of a science comes about in a way analogous to that in which a cathedral comes to be built as a result of the combined work of a number of individuals each applying their specialized skills. As J.R. Ravetz has put it, "Scientific knowledge is achieved by a complex social endeavour, and derives from the work of many craftsmen in their very special interaction with the world of nature".[4] A full objectivist characterization of a science would include a characterization of the skills and techniques that it involves.

An important general characteristic of the practice of physics since Galileo is the fact that it involves experiment. Experiment involves planned, theory-guided interference with nature. An artificial situation is constructed for the purpose of exploring and testing a theory. Experimental practice of this kind was absent from physics before Galileo. An important consequence of the fact that physics involves experiment in a basic way will be discussed in Chapter 13 and 14.

The details of the experimental techniques involved in physics have changed, of course, as physics has developed. The individual experimenter, when constructing his apparatus, judging the reliability of its functioning and using it to extract data will employ craft skills that he has learnt partly from textbooks but mainly by trial and error and interaction with more experienced colleagues. Whatever the confidence of the individual experimenter in the reliability of the results he produces, that subjective confidence will not be sufficient to qualify those results as constituting part of scientific knowledge. The results must be able to stand up to further testing procedures conducted, first, perhaps, by the experimenter's colleagues and later, if the social structure of science happens to be similar to that of our own, by the referees of journals. If the results survive such tests and become published, their adequacy will be liable to be tested on a wider front. It may turn out that the published results are discarded in the light of other experimental or theoretical developments. All this suggests that an experimental finding, whether it concerns the existence of a new fundamental particle, a new and more accurate estimate of the velocity of light, or whatever, is correctly seen as the product of a complex social activity rather than as the belief or possession of an individual.

Another general feature of modern physics that distinguishes it from physics before Galileo, and from many other bodies of knowledge, is the fact that, in the main, its theories are expressed in mathematical terms. A complete characterization of a science at some stage in its development would include a characterization of the theoretical and mathematical techniques involved. An example we have already encountered in this book is the method, introduced by Galileo, of splitting a vector into components and dealing with each separately. Another example is Fourier's technique of treating any wave form as a superposition of sine waves. A crucial difference between the wave theories of light put forward by Young and by Fresnel was the availability to the latter of the appropriate mathematics.[5]

An objectivist characterization of physics at some stage in its development, then, will include a specification of the theoretical propositions available for individual scientists to work on and the experimental and mathematical techniques available for them to work with.

4. Objectivism supported by Popper, Lakatos and Marx

The standpoint on knowledge that I, following Musgrave,[6] have referred to as objectivism was adopted, and indeed strongly advocated, by Popper and Lakatos. A book of essays by Popper is entitled, significantly, *Objective Knowledge*. A passage from that book reads:

> My . . . thesis involves the existence of two different senses of knowledge or of thought: (1) *knowledge or thought in the subjective sense,* consisting of a state of mind or of consciousness or a disposition to behave or to act, and (2) knowledge or thought in an objective sense, consisting of problems, theories, and arguments as such. Knowledge in this objective sense is totally independent of anybody's claim to know; it is also independent of anybody's belief, or disposition to assent; or to assert, or to act. Knowledge in the objective sense is *knowledge without a knower;* it is *knowledge without a knowing subject.*[7]

Lakatos fully supported Popper's objectivism and intended his methodology of scientific research programmes to constitute an objectivist account of science. He talked of "the cleavage between objective knowledge and its distorted reflections in individual minds"[8] and in a longer passage he observed,

> . . . a theory may be pseudoscientific even though it is eminently "plausible" and everybody believes it, and it may be scientifically valuable even if it is unbelievable and nobody believes it. A theory may even be of supreme scientific value even if no one *understands* it, let alone believes it.
>
> The cognitive value of a theory has nothing to do with its *psychological* influence on people's minds. Belief, commitment, understanding are states of the human mind . . . But the objective, scientific value of a theory . . . is independent of the human mind which creates it or understands it.[9]

Lakatos insisted that it was essential to adopt an objectivist position when writing the history of the internal development of a science. "A Popperian internal historian will not need to take any interest whatsoever in the *persons* involved, or in their beliefs about their own activities."[10] Consequently, a history of the internal development of a science will be "the history of disembodied science".[11]

In a sense historical materialism, the theory of society and social change initiated by Karl Marx, is an objectivist theory in which the objectivist approach that I have described with respect to knowledge is applied to society as a whole. Marx's objectivism is evident in his well-known remark, "It is not the consciousness of men that determines their being but, on the contrary, their social being that determines their consciousness."[12] From the materialist point of view individuals are born into some part of a pre-existing social structure that they do not choose and their consciousness is formed by what they do and experience in that structure. Although individuals may come to have some grasp of the nature of the social structure in which they live, there will always be "a cleavage between [the structure and workings of society] and its distorted reflections in individiaul minds". The outcome of the social actions of an individual will be determined by the details of the social situation and will typically be quite different from what the individual intended. Just as a physicist who attempts to contribute to the development of physics is confronted by an objective situation, which delimits the possibilities for choice and action and which influences the outcome of such action, so an individual who hopes to contribute to social change is confronted by an objective situation, which delimits the possibilities for choice and action and which influences the outcome of such choice and action. An analysis of the objective situation is as essential for an understanding of social change as it is for scientific change.

In the next chapter I will attempt to give an account of theory change in physics that is thoroughly objectivist.

FURTHER READING

The main sources for Popper's writings on objectivism are *Objective Knowledge* (Oxford: Oxford University Press, 1972), especially Chapters 3 and 4, and also Chapter 14 of his *The Open Society and its Enemies,* vol. 2 (London: Routledge and Kegan Paul, 1980). Popper's objectivism is summarized by A. Musgrave in his "The Objectivism of Popper's Epistemology", in *The Philosophy of Karl R. Popper,* ed. P.A. Schilpp (La Salle, Illinois: Open Court, 1974), pp.560-96. Popper's position is criticized by D. Bloor in "Popper's Mystification of Objective Knowledge", *Science Studies* 4 (1974): 65-76. Science as a social activity is usefully discussed in J.R. Ravetz, *Scientific Knowledge and its Social Problems* (Oxford: Oxford University Press, 1971); J. Ziman, *Public Knowledge* (Cambridge: Cambridge University Press, 1968); and Leslie Sklair, *Organized Knowledge* (St. Albans: Paladin, 1973). A more popular account, not primarily concerned with epistemological problems, is Bernard Dixon, *What is Science For?* (London: Collins, 1973). A version of Marxism which stresses the objectivist aspect and which contains some pointers towards an objectivist account of knowledge, is that defended by the contemporary French philosopher Louis Althusser. The most relevant of his works are *Reading Capital* (London: New Left Books, 1970) and *For Marx* (Harmondsworth: Allen Lane, 1969). Also of relevance in this connection is Dominique Lecourt, *Marxism and Epistemology* (London: New Left Books, 1975).

1. D.M. Armstrong, *Belief, Truth and Knowledge* (Cambridge: Cambridge University Press, 1973), p.137.
2. Classical rationalism should not be confused with the rationalism that I contrasted with relativism in the previous chapter. I hope these two somewhat different uses of the word rationalism do not lead to confusion.
3. For a defence of this controversial claim, see A.F. Chalmers, "The Limitations of Maxwell's Electromagnetic Theory", *Isis* 64 (1973): 469-83. For details of Maxwell's attempt to reduce electromagnetism to the mechanics of an aether, see A.F. Chalmers, "Maxwell's Methodology and His Application of It to Electromagnetism", *Studies in History and Philosophy of Science* 4 (1973): 107-64.

4. J.R. Ravetz, *Scientific Knowledge and Its Social Problems* (Oxford: Oxford University Press, 1971), p.81.
5. See John Worrall,"Thomas Young and the 'Refutation' of Newtonian Optics: A Case Study in the Interaction of Philosophy of Science and History of Science", in C. Howson, ed., *Method and Appraisal in The Physical Sciences* (Cambridge: Cambridge University Press, 1976), pp.107-79.
6. A. Musgrave, "The Objectivism of Popper's Epistemology", in *The Philosophy of Karl Popper,* ed. P.A. Schilpp, pp.560-96.
7. K.R. Popper, *Objective Knowledge* (Oxford: Oxford University Press, 1979), pp.108-9, italics in original.
8. I. Lakatos, "History of Science and its Rational Reconstructions", in *Boston Studies in the Philosophy of Science,* vol. 8, ed. R.C. Buck and R.S. Cohen (Dordrecht: Reidel Publ. Co. 1971), p.99.
9. J. Worrall and G. Currie, eds., *Imre Lakatos. Philosophical Papers Volume 1: The Methodology of Scientific Research Programmes* (Cambridge: Cambridge University Press, 1978), p.1, italics in original.
10. Lakatos, "History of Science and its Rational Reconstructions", p.127, italics in original.
11. Ibid., p.105.
12. Karl Marx, "A Contribution to the Critique of Political Economy", in *Karl Marx: Selected Works,* 2 vols. (Moscow: Co-operative Publishing Society, 1935), vol. 1, p.356.

11

An Objectivist Account of Theory Change in Physics

1. The limitations of Lakatos's objectivism

The account of theory change I wish to suggest is a modification of Lakatos's methodology of scientific research programmes.[1] Before presenting it I will, in this section, discuss the limitations of Lakatos's account of theory change, or rather explain why I do not think he has offered an account of theory change at all.

Lakatos's methodology involves the decisions and choices of scientists. They are involved in the adoption by scientists of a hardcore and positive heuristic. According to Lakatos, the hardcore of Newton's programme "is 'irrefutable' by the methodological decisions of its protagonists",[2] and a research programme has "a conventionally accepted (and thus by provisional decision, 'irrefutable') 'hard core' ".[3] The positive heuristic is a research policy or "preconceived plan"[4] which scientists choose to adopt. "Which problems scientists working in powerful research programmes rationally choose, is determined by the positive heuristic of the programme".[5]

A question that is important here is whether or not scientists are meant to be aware of the prescriptions contained in Lakatos's methodology. If they are not, then it is difficult to see how the methodology can *explain* scientific change. To simply note that changes in the history of physics have taken place in conformity with the methodology of scientific research programmes is not to explain why it has done so. On the other hand, if scientists are meant to act consciously in accordance with Lakatos's methodology then there are further problems. Firstly, it is difficult to see how scientists for the last two hundred years can have been aware of the prescriptions of a methodology that has only recently been devised. Lakatos himself has indicated the large gulf between the methodology Newton expressed and the one he followed in practice.[6] Secondly, Lakatos's methodology is not adequate for dictating the choices of scientists as we have seen, in keeping with his own declaration that his methodology was not intended to yield advice for scientists. Thirdly, any attempt to give an account of theory change that hinges in a crucial way on the conscious decisions and choices of scientists fails to take full heed of "the cleavage between objective knowledge . . . and its distorted reflections in individual minds".

An assumption that is made by Lakatos, as well as by Popper and Kuhn, is that theory change is to be explained by reference to the decisions and choices of scientists. Insofar as Lakatos and Popper fail to give adequate prescriptions for theory choice they fail to give an account of theory change, whilst Kuhn uncritically condones whatever choices are sanctioned by the scientific community. In the remainder of this chapter I will attempt to modify Lakatos's methodology in a way that avoids the conflation of theory choice and theory change.

2. Objective opportunities.

In section 2 of Chapter 10, I introduced the notion of an objective opportunity for development of a theory or programme. The account of theory change in physics that I wish to propose capitalizes on that notion. Given some theory and the associated practice at some stage in their joint development, a variety of opportunities for developing that theory will present themselves. Some lines of theoretical development will be possible by virtue of the theoretical and mathematical techniques available, whilst practical lines of development will be possible by virtue of the experimental techniques available. I will use the expression "degree of fertility" to describe the conglomeration of objective opportunities present in a research programme at some stage in its development. The degree of fertility of a programme at some juncture will be an objective property of that programme, which it possesses whether individual scientists realize it or not. It therefore differs from Lakatos's notion of a positive heuristic, which is a research policy more or less consciously adopted by scientists. The degree of fertility of a programme measures the extent to which it contains within it objective opportunities for development or the extent to which it opens up new lines of investigation.

A description by Stillman Drake of the extent to which Galileo's physics opened up lines of investigation captures the spirit of what is involved in degree of fertility. It reads,

> It was Galileo who, by consistently applying mathematics to physics and physics to astronomy, first brought mathematics, physics and astronomy together in a truly significant and fruitful way. The three disciplines had always been looked upon as essentially separate; Galileo revealed their triply paired relationships, and thereby opened new fields of investigation to men of widely divergent interests and abilities.[7]

Other illustrations can be drawn from case studies that have been made to support Lakatos's methodology. For example, drawing on E. Zahar's study of the eventual replacement of H.A. Lorentz's programme in electromagnetism by Einstein's special theory of relativity,[8] we can say that, in 1905, Einstein's theory possessed a greater degree of fertility than Lorentz's. Because Einstein's theory involved some very general assertions concerning the properties of space and time, opportunities presented themselves for exploring the consequences of those assertions in many areas of physics. By contrast, Lorentz's theory was firmly anchored in electromagnetic theory and could not be applied outside of it in a similar way. In his study of the competition between Young's wave theory and Newton's corpuscular theory of light, Worrall, referring to the situation in 1810, writes "because of the comparatively less developed state of the mechanics of elastic media relative to the mechanics of rigid particles, the heuristic of the corpuscular programme was . . . rather more definite than that of the wave programme".[9] The corpuscular theory possessed a higher degree of fertility than the wave programme in 1810.

It will help to clarify my notion of the degree of fertility characteristic of a programme if I attempt to answer some objections to it to which my attention has already been drawn. These are (i) the conception is too vague to allow for a quantitative measure of the degree of fertility of a programme, (ii) it has the unwelcome consequence that the more vague a theory or programme is, the greater will be its degree of fertility, since a sufficiently vague theory or programme will be compatible with virtually any line of development, (iii) degree of fertility is valueless as a tool for the historian since opportunities for development only come to light once they are taken advantage of, so that spelling out the degree of fertility of a programme amounts to no more than recording how it in fact developed, and (iv) degree of fertility is of no help in explaining the growth of science since the degree of fertility of a programme can be adequately analyzed and appreciated only with hindsight.

With respect to objection (i), I agree that it will not be possible to provide the means for constructing a quantitative measure of the degree of fertility of a programme. However, I do claim that it is often possible to make qualitative comparisons between the degrees of fertility of rival programmes, as the examples I have drawn from Lakatosian case studies indicate. This is all that is necessary to afford an objectivist account of theory change, as I hope to show.[10] Objection (ii), if it were valid, would certainly be devastating for my position. There are two reasons why it is not valid. Firstly, a vague course of action is not to be counted as an opportunity in the sense intended. An example of the latter must be specified precisely in terms of definite experimental, mathematical or theoretical techniques at the disposal of scientists at some historical juncture, together with specific theories and hypotheses constituting the hard core and protective belt of a programme at that juncture, and providing the raw material on which the aforementioned techniques can be brought to bear. The second reason why objection (ii) must be rejected is that the development, for which a theory with a high degree of fertility must provide many opportunities, is not any old development, but development towards novel predictions in something like Lakatos's sense.

Objection (iii) is best rebutted by giving examples of objective opportunities for development which, as a matter of fact, were not taken advantage of. Archimedes's physics provided opportunities for development that remained unheeded for centuries. In his work on the balance and centres of gravity and on hydrostatics he introduced techniques that could well have been extended to other areas and put to work on other existing raw material. For instance, the technique of formulating the fundamentals of a theory in an idealized, mathematical form treating of systems in mathematical, Euclidean space, a technique that he introduced in statics, could have been extended to dynamics, by considering moving levers as well as stationary ones, and objects falling through media as well as floating in them. It was not until Galileo that such opportunities were taken advantage of, by which time, of course, there was more theoretical raw material to work on than had been available to Archimedes.[11] The works of Ptolemy and Al Hazen provided opportunities for the development of optics that were not taken advantage of until the time of Galileo and Kepler. In his investigation of that problem, V. Ronchi, writes,

> Although we do not know who first invented spectacle lenses, we *do* know with some exactness when they were first introduced: somewhere between 1280 and 1285. Yet the first telescope did not appear until around 1590. Why did it take three whole centuries to put one spectacle lens in front of another?[12]

He then goes on to attempt to explain why this objective opportunity was not taken advantage of. Admittedly, in describing these objective opportunities use is made of material from history, physics and philosophy that was not available in the historical periods under investigation. Adequate characterization of objective opportunities and degrees of fertility are only possible with hindsight. In claiming this, objection (iv) is correct. However, far from being an objection to my position, the fact that scientists are not and need not be consciously aware of the degree of fertility of the programmes on which they work constitutes its strength. It is just this feature that makes possible an objectivist account of theory change that avoids the subjectivist elements present in the Lakatosian accounts.

3. An objectivist account of theory change in physics

Within important limits to be spelt out in the following section, I am now in a position to offer an objectivist account of theory change in modern physics. The account rests on a major assumption, namely, that in the society or societies in which physics is practised, there exist scientists with the appropriate skills, resources and frame of mind for developing that science. I need to be able to assume, for instance, that in those situations where an objectivist analysis reveals the existence of certain experimental or theoretical techniques, there will be scientists or groups of scientists with the mental and physical resources to put those techniques into practice. I presume that this assumption was satisfied in much of Europe for two hundred years or so of physics.

If my sociological assumption is satisfied, then we can presume that, if an objective opportunity for development of a programme is present, then sooner or later some scientist or group of scientists will take advantage of it. The net effect will be that a programme that offers more objective opportunities for development than its rival will tend to forge ahead of its rival as those opportunities are taken advantage of. This will be the case even if the majority of scientists happen to choose to work on the programme with the smaller degree of fertility. In the latter case, the minority choosing to work on the programme offering many opportunities for development will soon meet with success whilst the majority, those representing the majority view, will struggle in vain to take advantage of non-existent opportunities. Francois Jacob captures the spirit of my position when he writes,

> [In] this endless discussion between what is and what might be, in the quest for a chink revealing another possibility, the margin of freedom of the individual investigator is sometimes very narrow. The importance of the individual decreases as the number of practitioners increases: if an observation is not made here today, it will most frequently be made somewhere else tomorrow.[13]

My position can be illustrated by extending the analogy with nesting boxes that I used in Chapter 10 to illustrate the objective character of problem situations. We compare a garden in which there are a large number of nesting boxes with a second, otherwise similar garden, in which there are no nesting boxes. Given that the environment of each garden is suitably populated by birds then it is highly likely that after some months or years many more birds will have nested in the garden furnished with nesting boxes than in the other. This eventuality is adequately explained in terms of the objective opportunities for nesting offered by one garden as opposed to the other. The important point about this example for my purpose is that there will be no need to refer to the decisions of birds and the rationality or otherwise of those decisions in the explanation.

If my sociological assumption is satisfied, then, a programme with a high degree of fertility will tend to oust a programme with a lesser degree of fertility. However, a high degree of fertility is not alone sufficient to guarantee the success of a programme, for there can be no guarantee that opportunities, when pursued, will bear fruit. A programme with a high degree of fertility may come to nought nevertheless. An example is the vortex theory introduced by William Thomson, which aimed to explain the properties of atoms and molecules by representing them as vortices in a perfectly elastic, non-viscous aether. The degree to which that theory offered scope for development was strikingly described by Clerk Maxwell.[14] Nevertheless, pursuit of it did not lead to success and it was soon outstripped by programmes that met with more success. An objectivist account of theory-change, then, will need to take account, not only of the relative degrees of fertility of rival programmes, but also of their success in practice. Considerations of degree of fertility need to be augmented by an objectivist account of the extent to which rival programmes lead to novel predictions.

I have no special contribution to make to attempts to improve on accounts of novel predictions that appear in the literature.[15] I would like to point out, however, that there is an intimate link between novel predictions and degree of fertility. Confirmations of novel predictions can themselves result in the opening up of new avenues for future research, and therein lies part of their importance. For instance, when Hertz successfully produced radio waves, thereby confirming a novel prediction of Maxwell's electromagnetic theory, all sorts of new opportunities were brought into being, opportunities to investigate the properties of electromagnetic waves, to measure the velocity of light in new and more accurate ways, to develop microwaves as a new probe into the properties of matter, to open up a new area of astronomy and so on. An objectivist account of theory change would need to take heed of the extent to which programmes successfully led to the discovery of novel phenomena, and the extent to which those discoviers themselves offered objective opportunities for new avenues of exploration.

Programmes containing a coherent hard core which offers opportunities for development will in fact develop in a coherent way once those opportunities are taken up. The programme's degree of fertility will be further increased if that development leads to predictive successes. Lines of development that destroy the coherence of the hard core, and which consequently do not offer opportunities for development, will fizzle out for that reason. For example, the presence of the inverse square law as part of the hard core of Newton's theory is to be explained in terms of the degree of fertility stemming from that assumption and the successful predictions to which it led. By contrast, attempts to modify the programme by introducing a force law differing slightly from the inverse square law petered out because they offered no opportunities for coherent development, in spite of the fact that some scientists decided to modify the hard core in that way.[16] The continuity of science that Lakatos identifies in terms of the persistence of hard cores is thus explained by an appeal to the degree of fertility of programmes in a way that does not invoke the methodological decisions of scientists.

4. Some cautionary remarks

In this section I will try to protect my objectivist account of theory change in physics from some misinterpretations that experience has taught me are often attributed to it.

I have tried to give an account of theory change that does not hinge on the methodological decisions of scientists. In doing so I am certainly not suggesting that science somehow progresses of its own accord, without the intervention of humans. If the objective opportunities inherent in a programme within physics are to be taken advantage of, then this will be done by the application of the skills of individual scientists. Without them, physics would not even exist, let alone progress. In spite of this, if my account of theory change is correct, the process of theory change transcends the conscious intentions, choices and decisions of physicists. In particular, it is not determined by the *methodological* decisions of physicists. I do not claim, for example, that scientists should choose to work on the theory with the greatest degree of fertility, especially in view of the fact that a typical scientist will not be in a good position to appreciate all the opportunities for development offered by a theory or programme. My account of change assumes that, if an opportunity for development exists, some scientist or group of scientists will eventually take advantage of it, but it does not assume that any particular scientist or group will be aware of all of the opportunities for development. My account separates the problem of theory change from the problem of theory choice.

There is absolutely no guarantee that the sociological assumption, on which the objectivist account of theory change in physics depends, will always be satisfied. It was not satisfied in mediaeval Europe and there are strong grounds for believing that it is being undermined in contemporary society. It is likely that the way in which research funding is influenced by governments and industrial monopolies in contemporary society is such that some objective opportunities cannot be taken advantage of, so that the progress of physics is becoming increasingly controlled by factors external to physics. Nevertheless, my sociological assumption was roughly satisfied for two hundred or so years of physics and it is in that domain that I claim my account of theory change is applicable. If my sociological assumption is not satisfied then a very different account of theory change becomes necessary. I am not claiming to have offered an account of theory change in general.

The sociological assumption will never be completely satisfied.

The fine structure of the very short term progress of physics will inevitably involve such things as the personalities of scientists, the extent to which and the ways in which they communicate and so on. However, in the long term, provided there are scientists with the skills and resources available to take advantage of opportunities for development that do in fact exist, then I claim that the progress of physics will be explicable in terms of my account of theory change. The time scale appropriate for my objectivist account of theory change, and which distinugishes the long term from the short term, is that in which statements such as "Einstein's theory replaced Lorentz's" make sense.

FURTHER READING

C. Howson, *Method and Appraisal in the Physical Sciences* (Cambridge: Cambridge University Press, 1976) contains some excellent case studies in support of Lakatos's methodology. I claim that, suitably rewritten, they constitute support for my objectivist account of theory change.

1. The objectivist account of theory change outlined in this chapter has appeared previously in my "Towards An Objectivist Account of Theory Change", *British Journal for the Philosophy of Science* 30 (1979): 227-33 and in more detail in "An Improvement and a Critique of Lakatos's Methodology of Scientific Research Programmes", *Methodology and Science* 13 (1980): 2-27. I am grateful to the editors of those journals for permission to reproduce the material here.
2. I. Lakatos and A. Musgrave, *Criticism and the Growth of Knowledge* (Cambridge: Cambridge University Press, 1974), p.133.
3. I. Lakatos, "History of Science and Its Rational Reconstructions", in *Boston Studies in the Philosophy of Science,* vol. 8, ed. R.C. Buck and R.S. Cohen (Dordrecht: Reidel Publ. Co., 1971), p.99.
4. Ibid.
5. Lakatos and Musgrave (1974), p.137.
6. I. Lakatos, "Newton's Effect on Scientific Standards", in *Imre Lakatos. Philosophical Papers Volume 1: The Methodology of Scientific Research Programmes* (Cambridge: Cambridge University Press, 1978), pp.193-222. "The confusion, the poverty of Newton's *theory of scientific achievement* contrasts dramatically with the clarity, the richness of his *scientific achievement"*, p.220, italics in original. Gregory Currie has made the point that the decisions of scientists from the past must be explained by reference to how they appreciated the situation rather than in terms of some contemporary methodology, in his "The Role of Normative Assumptions in Historical Explanation", *Philosophy of Science* 47 (1980): 456-73.
7. Stillman Drake, *Galileo Studies* (Ann Arbor: University of Michigan Press, 1970), p.97.

8. Elie Zahar, "Why Did Einstein's Programme Supersede Lorentz's?", in *Method and Appraisal in the Physical Sciences,* ed. C. Howson (Cambridge: Cambridge University Press, 1976), pp.211-75.
9. John Worrall, "Thomas Young and the 'Refutation' of Newtonian Optics: a Case-study in the Interaction of Philosophy of Science and History of Science", *ibid.,* p.158. In the original the whole expression is in italics.
10. Insofar as degrees of fertility can only be compared but not individually measured, degree of fertility is in the same situation as a number of other notions in the philosophy of science, such as, for instance, Popper's degree of falsifiability. See K.R. Popper, *The Logic of Scientific Discovery* (London: Hutchinson, 1968), Ch.6.
11. For the relationships between the work of Archimedes and Galileo, see Maurice Clavelin, *The Natural Philosophy of Galileo* (Cambridge, Massachussetts: M.I.T. Press, 1974), Ch.3.
12. V. Ronchi, "The Influence of the Early Development of Optics on Science and Philosophy", in *Galileo: Man of Science,* ed. E. McMullin (New York: Basic Books, 1967), pp.195-206, italics in original.
13. Francois Jacob, *The Logic of Life: A History of Heredity* (New York: Vintage Books, 1976), p.11.
14. J.C. Maxwell, "Atom", in *The Scientific Papers of James Clerk Maxwell,* vol. 2, ed. W.D. Niven (New York: Dover, 1965), pp.445-84, esp. p.471.
15. For attempts to do so see Zahar, "Why Did Einstein's Programme Supersede Lorentz's?" and A. Musgrave, "Logical Versus Historical Theories of Confirmation", *British Journal For the Philosophy of Science* 25 (1974): 1-23.
16. Attempts to modify the hard core of Newton's programme are mentioned in A. Musgrave, "Method or Madness", *Essays in Memory of Imre Lakatos,* ed. R.S. Cohen, P.K. Feyerabend and M.W. Wartofsky (Dordrecht: Reidel Publ. Co., 1976), pp.457-91, esp. pp.464-73.

12

Feyerabend's Anarchistic Theory of Knowledge

One of the most challenging and provocative of contemporary accounts of science is the one that has been colourfully presented and defended by Paul Feyerabend, and no assessment of the nature and status of science would be complete without some attempt to come to terms with it. In this chapter I will summarize and assess what I take to be the key features of Feyerabend's position, mainly as it appears in his book *Against Method*.[1]

1. Anything goes

Feyerabend makes a strong case for the claim that none of the methodologies of science that have so far been proposed are successful. The main, although not the only, way in which he supports his claim is to show how those methodologies are incompatible with the history of physics. Many of his arguments against the methodologies which I have labelled inductivism and falsificationism resemble those that appear in the earlier chapters of this book. Indeed, the views expressed there owe some debt to Feyerabend's writings. Feyerabend convincingly argues that methodologies of science have failed to provide rules adequate for guiding the activities of scientists. Furthermore, he suggests that, given the complexity of history, it is most implausible to expect that science be explicable on the basis of a few simple methodological rules. To quote Feyerabend at some length,

> The idea that science can, and should, be run according to fixed and universal rules, is both unrealistic and pernicious. It is *unrealistic,* for it takes too simple a view of the talents of man and of the circumstances

which encourage, or cause, their development. And it is *pernicious* for the attempt to enforce the rules is bound to increase our professional qualifications at the expense of our humanity. In addition, the idea is *detrimental to science,* for its neglects the complex physical and historical conditions which influence scientific change. It makes science less adaptable and more dogmatic . . .

Case studies such as those reported in the preceding chapters . . . speak *against* the universal validity of any rule. All methodologies have their limitations and the only "rule" that survives is "anything goes".[2]

If methodologies of science are understood in terms of rules for guidance of the choices and decisions of scientists, then it seems to me that Feyerabend's position is correct. Given the complexity of any realistic situation within science and the unpredictability of the future as far as the development of a science is concerned, it is unreasonable to hope for a methodology that dictates that, given some situation, a rational scientist must adopt theory A, reject theory B or prefer theory A to theory B. Rules such as "adopt that theory which receives most inductive support from accepted facts" and "reject theories that are incompatible with generally accepted facts" are incompatible with those episodes in science that are commonly regarded as constituting its most progressive phases. Feyerabend's case against method hits at methodologies interpreted as providing rules for the guidance of scientists. Thus, he is able to welcome Lakatos as a fellow anarchist because his methodology does not provide rules for theory or programme choice. "The methodology of research programmes provides *standards* that aid the scientist in evaluating the historical situation in which he makes his decisions; it does not contain *rules* that tell him what to do."[3] Scientists, then, should not be constrained by the rules of the methodologist. In that sense, anything goes.

A passage from an article by Feyerabend written a decade before *Against Method* illustrates the fact that "anything goes" should not be interpreted it too wide a sense. In that passage, Feyerabend attempts to distinguish between the reasonable scientist and the crank.

The distinction does not lie in the fact that the former ["respectable" people] suggest what is plausible and promises success, whereas the latter [cranks] suggest what is implausible, absurd, and bound to fail. It *cannot* lie in this becase we never know in advance which theory will be successful and which theory will fail. It takes a long time to decide this question and every single step leading to such a decision is again open to revision . . . No, the distinction between the crank and the respectable thinker lies in the research that is done once a certain point of view is adopted. The crank usually is content with defending the point of view in its original, undeveloped, metaphysical form, and he is not at all prepared to test its usefulness in all those cases which seem to favour the opponent, or even to admit that their exists a problem. It is this further investigation, the details of it, the knowledge of the difficulties, of the general state of knowledge, the recognition of objections, which distinguishes the "respectable thinker" from the crank. The original content of his theory does not. If he thinks that Aristotle should be given a further chance, let him do it and wait for the results. If he rests content with this assertion and does not start elaborating a new dynamics, if he is unfamiliar with the initial difficulties of his position, then the matter is of no further interest. However, if he does not rest content with Aristotelianism in the form in which it exists today but tries to adapt it to the present situation in astronomy, physics, and microphysics, making new suggestions, looking at old problems from a new point of view, then be grateful that there is at last somebody who has unusual ideas and do not try to stop him in advance with irrelevant and misguided arguments.[4]

In brief, if one is to make a contribution to physics, for example, one need not become familiar with contemporary methodologies of science, but one will need to become familiar with some physics. It will not be sufficient merely to follow one's whims and inclinations in an uninformed way. It is not the case that, in science, anything goes in an unrestricted sense.

Feyerabend successfully argues against method insofar as he has shown that it is not advisable for the choices and decisions of scientists to be constrained by the rules laid down by or implicit in methodologies of science. However, if the strategy of the previous chapter is adopted, separating the problem of theory change from the problem of theory choice, problems concerning rules for guiding theory choice do not constitute problems for an account of theory change. I suggest my account of theory change in physics is immune from Feyerabend's critique of method.

2. Incommensurability

An important component of Feyerabend's analysis of science is his view on incommensurability, which has something in common with Kuhn's view on the matter referred to in Chapter 8.[5] Feyerabend's conception of incommensurability stems from what I have referred to in Chapter 3 as theory-dependence of observation. The meanings and interpretations of concepts and the observation statements that employ them will depend on the theoretical context in which they occur. In some cases the fundamental principles of two rival theories may be so radically different that it is not possible even to formulate the basic concepts of one theory in terms of the other with the consequence that the two rivals do not share any observation statements. In such cases it is not possible to compare the rival theories logically. It will not be possible to logically deduce some of the consequences of one theory from the tenets of its rival for the purposes of comparison. The two theories will be incommensurable.

One of Feyerabend's examples of incommensurability is the relationship between classical mechanics and relativity theory. According to the former — interpreted realistically, that is, as attempting to describe how the world, both observable and unobservable, really is[6] — physical objects have shape, mass and volume. Those properties exist in physical objects and can be changed as a result of physical interference. In relativity theory, interpreted realistically, properties such as shape, mass and volume no longer exist, but become relations between objects and a reference frame and can be changed, without any physical interaction, by changing from one reference frame to another. Consequently, any observation statement referring to physical objects within classical mechanics will have a different meaning to a similar looking observation statement in relativity theory. The two theories are incommensurable and cannot be compared by comparing their logical consequences. To quote Feyerabend himself,

> The new conceptual system that arises (within relativity theory) does not just *deny* the existence of classical states of affairs, it does not even permit us to formulate *statements* expressing such states of affairs. It does not, and cannot, share a single statement with its predecessor — assuming all the time that we do not use the theories as classificatory schemes for the ordering of neutral facts . . . the positivist scheme of progress with its "Popperian spectacles", breaks down.[7]

Other pairs of incommensurable theories mentioned by Feyerabend include quantum mechanics and classical mechanics, impetus theory and Newtonian mechanics, and materialism and mind-body dualism.

It does not follow from the fact that a pair of rival theories are incommensurable that they cannot be compared in any way. One way of comparing such a pair of theories is to confront each of them with a series of observable situations and to keep a record of the degree to which each of the rival theories is compatible with those situations, interpreted in its own terms. Other ways of comparing theories referred to by Feyerabend involve considerations of whether they are linear or non-linear, coherent or incoherent, whether they are daring or safe approximations and so on.[8]

If we are concerned with the problem of theory choice, then a problem arises concerning which of the several criteria of comparison are to be preferred in situations where the criteria conflict. According to Feyerabend, the choice between criteria and, consequently, the choice between incommensurable theories is ultimately subjective.

> Transition to criteria not involving content thus turns theory choice from a "rational" and "objective" and rather one-dimensional routine into a complex discussion involving conflicting preferences, and propaganda will play a major role in it, as it does in all cases involving preferences.[9]

In Feyerabend's view, incommensurability, although it does not remove all means of comparing rival incommensurable theories, leads to a necessarily subjective aspect of science.

> What remains [after we have removed the possibility of logically comparing theories by comparing sets of deductive consequences] are aesthetic judgements, judgements of taste, metaphysical prejudices, religious desires, in short, *what remains are our subjective wishes.*[10]

I accept Feyerabend's view that some rival theories cannot be compared by merely logical means. However, I suggest that his drawing of subjectivist consequences from this fact needs to be countered in a number of ways. If we are to focus on the issue of theory choice, then I am prepared to admit that there will be some subjective element involved when a scientist chooses to adopt or work on one theory rather than another, although those choices will be influenced by "external" factors such as career prospects and availability of funds in addition to the kinds of consideration mentioned by Feyerabend in the above quotations. However, I think it needs to be said that, although individual judgements and wishes are in a sense subjective and cannot be determined by logically compelling arguments, this does not mean that they are immune to rational argument. The preferences of individuals can be criticized, for example, by showing that they are seriously inconsistent or by showing that they have consequences that the individual holding them would not welcome.[11] I am aware that the preferences of individuals are not solely determined by rational argument and am aware that they will be strongly moulded and influenced by the material conditions in which the individual exists and acts. (A major change in career prospects is likely to have a greater effect on an individual's preferences than a rational argument, to give a superficial example.) Nevertheless, the subjective judgements and wishes of individuals are not sacrosanct and are not simply given. They are open to criticism and to change by argument and by alteration of the material conditions. Feyerabend welcomes his conclusion that science contains a subjective element because it offers the scientist a degree of freedom absent from the "more pedestrian parts" of science.[12] I will have more to say about Feyerabend's conception of freedom in a later section.

My second kind of response to Feyerabend's remarks on incommensurability takes us away from the issue of theory choice. Zahar's case study of the rivalry between Lorentz's and Einstein's theories, suitably modified in the light of my objectivist account of theory change, explains how and why Einstein's theory eventually replaced Lorentz's. The explanation is in terms of the extent to which Einstein's theory offered more objective opportunities for development than Lorentz's, and the extent to which those opportunities bore fruit when taken advantage of. That explanation is possible in spite of the fact that the theories are at least in part incommensurable in Feyerabend's sense,[13] although it is not subjectivist. It must be conceded that subjective decisions and choices will be involved in the conditions specified by the sociological assumption on which my objectivist account of theory change depends. The account assumes that there are scientists with the appropriate skills and resources to take advantage of opportunities for development that present themselves. Different scientists and groups of scientists may make different choices when responding to the same situation, but my account of theory change does not depend on the individual preferences guiding those choices.

3. Science not necessarily superior to other fields

Another important aspect of Feyerabend's view of science concerns the relationship between science and other forms of knowledge. He points out that many methodologists take for granted, without argument, that science (or, perhaps, physics) constitutes the paradigm of rationality. Thus Feyerabend writes of Lakatos,

> Having finished his "reconstruction" of modern science, he [Lakatos] turns it against other fields *as if it had already been established* that

modern science is superior to magic or to Aristotelian science, and that it has no illusory results. However, there is not a shred of an argument of this kind. "Rational reconstructions" take "basic scientific wisdom" *for granted,* they do not *show* that it is better than the "basic wisdom" of witches and warlocks.[14]

Feyerabend complains, with justification, that defenders of science typically judge it to be superior to other forms of knowledge without adequately investigating those other forms. He observes that "critical rationalists" and defenders of Lakatos have examined science in great detail but that their "attitude towards Marxism or astrology, or other traditional heresies is very different. Here the most superficial examination and most shoddy arguments are deemed sufficient".[15] He backs up his claim with examples.

Feyerabend is not prepared to accept the necessary superiority of science over other forms of knowledge. Further, in the light of his incommensurability thesis, he rejects the idea that there ever can be a decisive argument in favour of science over other forms of knowledge incommensurable with it. If science is to be compared with other forms of knowledge then it will be necessary to investigate the nature, aims and methods of science and those other forms of knowledge. This will be done by the study of "historical records — textbooks, original papers, records of meetings and private conversations, letters and the like".[16] It cannot even be assumed, without further investigation, that a form of knowledge under investigation must conform to the rules of logic as they are usually understood by contemporary philosophers and rationalists. Failure to conform to the demands of classical logic may well be, but is not necessarily, a fault. An example offered by Feyerabend concerns modern quantum mechanics. To consider the question whether the modes of reasoning involved in some version of that theory violate the dictates of classical logic or not, it is necessary to investigate quantum mechanics and the way in which it functions. Such an investigation may reveal a new kind of logic operating which can be shown to have certain advantages, in the context of quantum mechanics, over more traditional logic. On the other hand, of course, the discovery of violations of logic *may* constitute a serious criticism of quantum mechanics. This would be the case, for example, if contradictions were discovered that had undesirable consequences; for example, if it were discovered that for every event predicted by the theory, the denial of that event is also predicted. I do not think Feyerabend would disagree with this latter point, but neither do I think he gives it due emphasis.

Once again, I can accept a substantial part of Feyerabend's views on the comparison of physics with other forms of knowledge. If we wish to know what the aims and methods of a form of knowledge are and the extent to which it has accomplished those aims, we need to study that form of knowledge. I can even support Feyerabend's point with an example of my own. Although it is somewhat a caricature of the history of philosophy, it can be said that for two thousand years prior to Galileo, philosophers argued about the question of whether or not mathematical theories are applicable to the physical world, the Platonists giving an affirmative answer and the Aristotelians a negative one. Galileo settled the issue, not by producing a decisive philosophical argument but by doing it. We learn about the way in which it is possible to characterize some aspects of the physical world by analyzing physics since Galileo. To understand the, perhaps changing, nature of physics, we need to investigate physics, whilst to understand other forms of knowledge we will need to investigate those other forms. It is illegitimate, for example, to reject Marxism on the grounds that it does not conform to some preconceived notion of the scientific method, as Popper does, or to defend it on similar grounds, as Althusser does.

Although I agree with Feyerabend's basic point here, the use to which I would wish to put it is somewhat different. The false assumption that there is a universal scientific method to which all forms of knowledge should conform plays a detrimental role in our society here and now, especially in the light of the fact that the version of the scientific method usually appealed to is some crude empiricist or inductivist one. This is especially true in the domain of social theory, when theories that serve to manipulate aspects of our society at a superficial level (market research, behaviourist psychology), rather than serving to understand it and helping us to change it at some deeper level, are defended in the name of science. Rather than focusing on what seem to me to be pressing social problems such as these, Feyerabend contrasts science with Voodoo, astrology and the like, and argues that the latter cannot be ruled out by recourse to some general criterion of scientificity and rationality. There are two reasons why I am unhappy with this emphasis. The first is that I am not convinced that a detailed study of Voodoo or astrology would reveal that they have well-defined aims and methods of achieving those aims, although, since I have not carried out the analysis, I must admit that this is somewhat a prejudice. Certainly, nothing that Feyerabend has written encourages me to change my mind. The second reason is that the status of

Voodoo, astrology and the like is not a pressing problem in our society, here and now. We are simply not in a position to have a "free choice" between science and Voodoo, or Western rationality and that of the Nuer tribe.

4. Freedom of the individual

Much of Feyerabend's thesis in *Against Method* is negative. It involves the denial of the claim that there is a method capable of accounting for the history of physics, and that the superiority of physics over other forms of knowledge can be established by appeal to some scientific method. However, there is a positive side to Feyerabend's case. Feyerabend defends what he refers to as the "humanitarian attitude". According to that attitude, individual humans should be free and possess liberty in something like the sense John Stuart Mill defended in his essay "On Liberty". Feyerabend is in favour of "the attempt to increase liberty, to lead a full and rewarding life" and supports Mill in advocating "the cultivation of individuality which alone produces, or can produce, well-developed human beings".[17] From this humanitarian point of view, Feyerabend's anarchistic view of science gains support because, within science, it increases the freedom of individuals by encouraging the removal of all methodological constraints, whilst in a broader context it encourages a freedom for individuals to choose between science and other forms of knowledge.

From Feyerabend's point of view the institutionalization of science in our society is inconsistent with the humanitarian attitude. In schools, for example, science is taught as a matter of course. "Thus, while an American can now choose the religion he likes, he is still not permitted to demand that his children learn magic rather than science at school. There is a separation between state and Church, there is no separation between state and science".[18] What we need to do in the light of this, writes Feyerabend, is to "free society from the strangling hold of an ideologically petrified science just as our ancestors freed *us* from the strangling hold of the One True Relgion!"[19] In Feyeraband's image of a free society science will not be given preference over other forms of knowledge or other traditions. A mature citizen in a free society is "a person who has learned to make up his mind and who has then *decided* in favour of what he thinks suits him best". Science will be studied as a historical phenomenon "together with other fairy tales such as the myths of 'primitive' societies" so that each individual "has the information needed for arriving at a free decision".[20] In Feyerabend's ideal society the state is ideologically neutral. Its function is to orchestrate the struggle between ideologies to ensure that individuals maintain freedom of choice and do not have an ideology imposed on them against their will.[21]

The notion of liberty and freedom of the individual that Feyerabend has taken over from Mill is open to a standard objection. That notion, which views freedom as freedom from all constraint, overlooks the positive half of the issue, namely, the possibilities within a social structure to which individuals have access. For example, if we analyze freedom of speech in our society solely in terms of freedom from censorship, we overlook issues such as the extent to which various individuals have access to the media. The eighteenth century philosopher, David Hume, nicely illustrated the point I am getting at when he criticized John Locke's idea of the Social Contract. Locke had construed the social contract as being freely adopted by members of a democratic society and argued that anyone not wishing to subscribe to the contract was free to emigrate. Hume replied,

> Can we seriously say, that a poor peasant or artisan has a free choice to leave his country, when he knows no foreign language or manners, and lives from day to day, by the small wages which he acquires? We may as well assert that a man, by remaining in a vessel, freely consents to the domination of the master; though he was carried on board while asleep, and must leap into the ocean and perish, the moment he leaves her.[22]

Each individual is born into a society that pre-exists and, in that sense, is not freely chosen. The freedom an individual possesses will depend on the position he occupies in the social structure, so that an analysis of social structure is a pre-requisite for an understanding of freedom of the individual. There is at least one place in *Against Method* where Feyerabend indicates that he is aware of this kind of point. In a footnote to a remark about freedom of research he notes:

> The scientist is still restricted by the properties of his instruments, the amount of money available, the intelligence of his assistants, the attitudes of his colleagues, his playmates — he or she, is restricted by innumerable physical, physiological, sociological, historical constraints.[23]

Feyerabend's subsequent talk of freedom of the individual fails to give adequate attention to the constraints operating in society. Just as a scientist hoping to make a contribution to science is faced with an objective situation, so an individual hoping to improve society is faced with an objective social situation. Further, just as a scientist in a given situation will have at his disposal a range of theoretical and experimental techniques, so a social reformer in a particular social situation will have access to a set of political techniques. In both kinds of situation the actions and aspirations of the individual can be adequately assessed and analyzed only with respect to the raw materials that are to be worked on and the "tools" or "means of production" available.[24] If we are to change contemporary society for the better then we have no alternative but to start with the society we are confronted with and to attempt to change it by means that present themselves. From this point of view Feyerabend's utopian ideal of a free society is of no help.

What can easily be seen, and in my experience frequently is seen, as the message of Feyerabend's recent writings, is that everyone should follow their individual inclinations and do their own thing. If this view is adopted, it is liable to lead to a situation in which those who already have access to power will keep it. As John Krige has put it, in a way that I wish I had thought of myself, *"anything goes . . .* means that, in practice, *everything stays"*.[25]

FURTHER READING

In *Science in a Freely Society* (London: New Left Books, 1978), Feyerabend develops further some of the ideas of *Against Method* and responds to some of his critics. A useful short article that presents the essence of Feyerabend's position is "How to Defend Society Against Science", *Radical Philosophy* 11 (1975): 3-8. In general, the critiques of Feyerabend's position that have appeared in the literature are not of a high standard. The extreme individualism that can be read into Feyerabend's writings, some of it with justification, is strongly criticized from an Althusserian Marxist perspective in J. Curthoys and W. Suchting, "Feyerabend's Discourse Against Method: A Marxist Critique", *Inquiry* 20 (1977): 243-397.

1. Paul Feyerabend, *Against Method: Outline of an Anarchistic Theory of Knowledge* (London: New Left Books, 1975).
2. Ibid., pp.295-96, italics in original.
3. Ibid., p.196, italics in original.

4. Paul Feyerabend, "Realism and Instrumentalism: Comments on the Logic of Factual Support", in *The Critical Approach to Science and Philosophy,* ed. M. Bunge (New York: Free Press, 1964), p.305, italics in original. Feyerabend is not always happy with those critics who assume that he still subscribes to what he has written in the past. (See *Against Method,* p.114.) I do not much care whether Feyerabend still accepts the message of the passage quoted or not. Apart from some misgivings about the individualist orientation of the passage, I certainly accept it and, more importantly, none of the arguments in *Against Method* tell against it.

5. Feyerabend discusses the relationship between his own and Kuhn's views in his "Changing Patterns of Reconstruction", *British Journal for the Philosophy of Science* 28 (1977): 351-82, section 6. The other main source for Feyerabend's views on incommensurability is *Against Method,* Ch. 17.

6. Realism will be discussed in the next chapter.

7. *Against Method*, p.275-76, italics in original.

8. "Changing Patterns of Reconstruction", p.365, n.2.

9. Ibid., p.366.

10. *Against Method,* p.285, italics in original.

11. If an individual whose preferences are so criticized responds by insisting that he does not mind if his preferences are seriously inconsistent and, in addition, has no response to the usual objections to inconsistencies, I, for one, see no reason why that individual's views should be taken seriously. Feyerabend's own distinction between cranks and "respectable" thinkers is relevant here.

12. *Against Method,* p.285.

13. Although Feyerabend does not list this pair of theories as examples of incommensurable ones, he seems committed to the fact that they are so in view of the fact that Lorentz's theory incorporates classical mechanics, and the classical conception of space, time and mass.

14. *Against Method,* p.205, italics in original.

15. P. Feyerabend, "On the Critique of Scientific Reason", in *Method and Appraisal in the Physical Sciences,* ed. C. Howson, p.315, n.9.

16. *Against Method,* p.253.

17. Ibid., p.20.

18. Ibid., p.299.

19. Ibid., p.307.

20. Ibid., p.308, italics in original.

21. Feyerabend's ideal of a free society is touched on in *Against Method,* but developed in more detail in his *Science in a Free Society* (London: New Left Books, 1978).

22. The quotation from Hume's "Of the Original Contract" is in E. Barker, *Social Contract: Essays by Locke, Hume and Rousseau* (London: Oxford University Press, 1976), p.156. The specific views of Locke criticized in the passage can be found on pp.70-72 of the same volume.

23. *Against Method,* p.187.

24. Louis Althusser has made a useful analogy between material production and other forms of production such as the production of knowledge and the production of social change. See, especially his *For Marx* (Harmondsworth: Allen Lane, 1969), Ch. 6.

25. John Krige, *Science, Revolution and Discontinuity* (Brighton, Sussex: Harvester, 1980), p.142, italics in original.

13

Realism, instrumentalism and truth

1. Introductory remarks

In this and the following chapter I will attempt to deal with some problematic questions concerning the relationship between scientific theories and the world to which they are meant to apply. On the one hand we have scientific theories that are human constructions and that are subject to, perhaps endless, change and development. On the other hand we have the world to which those theories are meant to apply and whose mode of behaviour, in the case of the physical world at least, is not subject to change. What is the relationship between the two domains?

One kind of answer to this question is that theories do, or aim to, describe what the world is really like. I will use the term "realism" to characterize positions that adopt a version of this answer. From the realist point of view the kinetic theory of gases describes what gases are really like. The kinetic theory is interpreted as claiming that gases really are made up of molecules in random motion colliding with each other and with the walls of the containing vessel. Similarly, from a realist point of view, classical electromagnetic theory is interpreted as claiming that there really are electric and magnetic fields in the world that obey Maxwell's equations and charged particles that obey the Lorentz force equation.

According to an alternative view, which I will call instrumentalism, the theoretical component of science does not describe reality. Theories are understood as instruments designed to relate one set of observable states of affairs with others. For the instrumentalist, the moving molecules referred to by the kinetic theory of gases are convenient fictions enabling scientists to relate and make predictions about observable manifestations of the properties of gases, whilst the fields and charges of electromagnetic theory are fictions enabling scientists to do likewise for magnets, electrified bodies and current-carrying circuits.

Realism typically involves the notion of truth. For the realist, science aims at *true* descriptions of what the world is really like. A theory that correctly describes some aspect of the world and its mode of behaviour is true, whilst a theory that incorrectly describes some aspect of the world and its mode of behaviour is false. According to realism, as typically construed, the world exists independently of us as knowers, and is the way it is independently of our theoretical knowledge of it. True theories correctly describe that reality. If a theory is true, it is true because the world is the way it is. Instrumentalism will also typically involve a notion of truth but in a more restricted way. Descriptions of the observable world will be true or false according to whether or not they correctly describe it. However, the theoretical constructs, that are designed to give us instrumental control of the observable world, will not be judged in terms of truth or falsity but rather in terms of their usefulness as instruments.

The idea that science aims at a true characterization of reality is often used as a counter to relativism. Popper, for example, uses truth in this way. According to that usage, a theory can be true even though nobody believes it and can be false even if everybody believes it. True theories, if they are indeed true, are not true relative to the beliefs of individuals or groups. Truth, understood as a correct characterization of reality, is objective truth for realists such as Popper.

Later in this chapter I will argue that the notion of truth typically incorporated into realism is problematic. Before doing that I will take a more detailed look at instrumentalism and show how, on the face of it, realism seems to have distinct advantages over it.

2. Instrumentalism

Instrumentalism in its extreme form involves a sharp distinction between concepts applicable to observable situations and theoretical concepts. The aim of science is to produce theories that are convenient devices or instruments for connecting one set of observable situations with another. Descriptions of the world involving observable entities do describe what the world is really like, but descriptions of systems involving theoretical concepts do not.

The latter are to be understood as useful fictions facilitating our calculations. Some simple examples will illustrate the instrumentalist position. The naive instrumentalist will admit that there really are billiard-balls in the world and that they can roll at various velocities, colliding with each other and with the sides of a billiard-table, which also really exists. Newtonian mechanics is to be regarded in this context as a calculating device, enabling the observable positions and velocities of the billiard-balls at some instant of time to be deduced from their observable positions and speeds at some different time. The forces involved in these and similar calculations (the impulsive forces due to impact, frictional forces, etc.) are not to be taken as entities that really exist. They are inventions of the physicist. In a similar way, the atoms and molecules involved in the kinetic theory of gases are also regarded by our instrumentalist as convenient theoretical fictions. The introduction of these theoretical entities is to be justified by their usefulness in connecting one set of observations of a physical system involving gases (the height of the mercury in a manometer, the reading of a thermometer, etc.) with another similar set. Scientific theories are nothing more than sets of rules for connecting one set of observable phenomena with another. Ammeters, iron filings, planets and light rays exist in the world. Electrons, magnetic fields, Ptolemaic epicycles and the aether need not.

Whether there are things existing in the world besides observable things, which are perhaps responsible for the behaviour of observable things, need not concern the naive instrumentalist. Whatever his position on this question, for him it is not the business of science to establish what may exist beyond the realm of observation. Science provides no sure means of bridging the gap between the observable and the unobservable.

Discussions from the earlier parts of this book provide ample material for criticism of this naive variety of instrumentalism. Perhaps the most fundamental criticism of it strikes at the strong distinction that the instrumentalist makes between observational and theoretical entities. The fact that all observational terms are theory-laden was supported at length in Chapter 3. Planets, light rays, metals and gases are all concepts that are theoretical to some degree, and acquire their meaning at least in part from the theoretical network in which they figure. The velocities that the instrumentalist was happy to ascribe to billiard-balls in our earlier example are instances of a particularly sophisticated theoretical concept involving the idea of a mathematical limit, which took a great deal of ingenuity and labour to develop. Even the concept of a billiard-ball implies theoretical properties such as individuality and rigidity. Insofar as instrumentalists share with inductivists a cautious attitude, which encourages them to assert nothing other than can safely be derived from the sure basis of observation, their position is undermined by the fact that all observation statements are theory dependent and fallible. The naive instrumentalist position rests on a distinction that is not adequate for the task demanded of it.

The fact that theories can lead to novel predictions is an embarrassment for instrumentalists. It must seem a strange kind of accident to them that theories, that are supposed to be mere calculating devices, can lead to the discovery of new kinds of observable phenomena by way of concepts that are theoretical fictions. The development of theories concerning the molecular structure of organic chemical compounds provides a nice example. The idea that the molecular structure of some compounds, benzene for instance, should consist of closed rings of atoms was first proposed by Kekulé. Kekulé himself had a somewhat instrumentalist attitude towards his theory and regarded his ring structures as useful theoretical fictions. On this view, it must be regarded as a remarkable coincidence that these theoretical fictions can nowadays be seen almost "directly" through electron microscopes. Likewise, instrumentalist defenders of the kinetic theory of gases should have been somewhat taken aback to observe the results of collisions of their theoretical fictions with smoke particles in the phenomenon of Brownian motion. Finally, Hertz himself reported that he had been able to produce the fields of Maxwell's electromagnetic theory in a "visible and almost tangible form". Episodes such as these undermine the naive instrumentalist claim that theoretical entities have a fictitious or unreal existence in a way that observable entities do not. Further difficulties with instrumentalism will come to light in section 4.

In so far as they are prepared to conjecture that the theoretical entities of their theories correspond to what really exists in the world, realists are more speculative and bold and less cautious and defensive than instrumentalists. In the light of this, and of the discussion of the superiority of the falsificationist over the inductivist view of science in Chapters 4 and 5, we might expect the realist stance to be more productive than the instrumentalist stance. That this is indeed the case will be supported by an historical example.

Some contemporaries of Copernicus and Galileo took an instrumentalist attitude to the Copernican theory. Osiander, the author of the preface to Copernicus's main work, *The Revolutions of the Heavenly Spheres,* wrote:

> . . . it is the duty of an astronomer to compose the history of the celestial motions through careful and skilful observation. Then turning to the causes of these motions or hypotheses about them, he must conceive and devise, since he cannot in any way attain to the true causes, such hypotheses as, being assumed, enable the motions to be calculated correctly from the principles of geometry, for the future as well as the past. The present author [Copernicus] has performed both these duties excellently. For these hypotheses need not be true nor even probable; if they provide a calculus consistent with the observations that alone is sufficient.[1]

That is, the Copernican theory is not to be taken as a description of what the world is really like. It does not assert that the earth really moves around the sun. Rather, it is a calculating device enabling one set of observable planetary positions to be connected with other sets. The calculations become easier if the planetary system is treated *as if* the sun were at the centre.

By contrast, Galileo was a realist. As he rose from his knees having confessed before the Roman Inquisition of the "errors of his ways" in defending the Copernican system, he is alleged to have tapped the ground beneath him and to have muttered, "And yet, it moves." For a realist defender of the Copernican theory, the earth really moves around the sun.

The supporters of Osiander had good reasons for taking their instrumentalist line. By doing so, they certainly avoided the controversies that raged around the clash between the Copernican theory on the one hand and contemporary Christianity and Aristotelian metaphysics on the other. There were also physical arguments against the Copernican system, as discussed in Chapter 6, and an instrumentalist interpretation of the theory protected it from those difficulties. By contrast, the realist position defended by Galileo posed many problems. It was just those problems that provided a major incentive for the development of a more adequate optics and a more adequate mechanics. As our earlier study demonstrated, it was the realist attitude that was productive, at least in this case. Even if the Copernican theory had failed to prove capable of overcoming its inadequacies, much would have been learnt about optics and mechanics in the process. The realist attitude is to be preferred to the naive instrumentalist one because it opens up more opportunities for development.

3. The correspondence theory of truth

As indicated in section 1, the typical realist position incorporates a notion of truth in such a way that true theories can be said to give a correct description of some aspect of the real world. In this section I will investigate attempts that have been made to make more precise the notion of truth operative in this connection. Although I will not argue it here, I take it that the so-called "correspondence theory of truth" is the only viable contender for an account of truth able to fulfil the demands of the realist, and I will restrict myself to discussion and criticism of that theory.

The general idea of the correspondence theory of truth seems straightforward enough and can be illustrated by examples from common discourse in a way that makes it appear almost trivial. According to the correspondence theory a sentence is true if it corresponds to the facts. Thus the sentence "the cat is on the mat" is true if it corresponds to the facts, that is, if there is indeed a cat on the mat, whilst the sentence is false if there is no cat on the mat. A sentence is true if things are as the sentence says they are and false otherwise.

One difficulty with the notion of truth is the ease with which use of it can lead to paradoxes. The so-called liar paradox provides an example. If I say "I never tell the truth" then if what I have said is true, then what I have said is false. Another well known example goes as follows: We imagine a card, on one side of which is written "The sentence written on the other side of this card is true", while on the other side of the card is written, "The sentence written on the other side of this card is false". It is not difficult to see how, given this situation, one can arrive at the paradoxical conclusion that either sentence on the card is both true and false.

The logician Alfred Tarski demonstrated how, for a particular language system, paradoxes can be avoided. The crucial step was his insistence that, when one is talking of the truth or falsity of the sentences in some language system, one must carefully and systematically distinguish sentences in the language system that is being talked about, the "object language", from sentences in the language system in which talk about the object language is carried out, the "metalanguage". Referring to the paradox involving the card, if we adopt Tarski's theory then we must decide whether the sentences on the card are within the language system being talked about or within the language system in which the talking is being done. If the sentences on both sides of the card are taken to be in the object language then they cannot also be taken as referring to each other. If one follows the rule that each of the sentences must be in either the object language or the metalanguage but not in both, so that neither sentence can both refer to the other and be referred to by the other, then no paradoxes arise.

A key idea of Tarski's correspondence theory, then, is that if we are to talk about truth for the sentences of a particular language, then we need a more general language, the metalanguage, in which we can refer both to the sentences of the object language and to the facts with which those object language sentences are intended to correspond. Tarski needed to be able to show how the correspondence notion of truth can be systematically developed for all sentences within the object language in a way that avoids paradoxes. The reason that this was a technically difficult task is that for any interesting language there is an infinite number of sentences. Tarski achieved his task for languages involving a finite number of single placed predicates, that is, predicates such as "is white" or "is a table". His technique involved taking as given what it means for a predicate to be satisfied by an object, x. Examples from everyday language sound trivial. For instance, the predicate "is white" is satisfied by object x, if and only if, x is white and the predicate "is a table" is satisfied by x, if and only if, x is a table. Given this notion of satisfaction for all the predicates of a language, Tarski showed how the notion of truth can be built up from this starting point for all the sentences of the language. To use technical terminology, taking the notion of primitive satisfaction as given, Tarski defined truth recursively.

Tarski's result was certainly of major technical importance for mathematical logic. It had a fundamental bearing on model theory and also had ramifications for proof theory. It also showed why it is that contradictions can occur when truth is discussed in natural languages and indicated how such contradictions can be avoided. Did Tarski achieve more than this? In particular, did he go any way towards explicating the notion of truth in a way that might help us to understand the claim that truth is the aim of science? Tarski himself did not think so. He regarded his account as "epistemologically neutral". Others have not shared Tarski's view. Popper, for example, writes, "Tarski . . . rehabilitated the correspondence theory of absolute or objective truth which had become suspect. He vindicated the free use of the intuitive idea of truth as correspondence to the facts".[2] Let us look at Popper's use of Tarski to see if he (Popper) is able to sustain the claim that it is meaningful to talk of truth as the aim of science.

Here is an attempt by Popper to elucidate the idea of "correspondence to the facts".

> . . . we shall first consider the following two formulations, each of which states very simply (in a metalanguage) under what conditions a certain assertion (of an object language) corresponds to the facts.
> 1. The statement, or the assertion, "snow is white" corresponds to the facts if, and only if, snow is, indeed, white.
> 2. The statement, or the assertion, "grass is red" corresponds to the facts if, and only if, grass is, indeed, red.[3]

This is all Popper really has to offer by way of an attempt to articulate what it means to say of a scientific claim that it is true or that it corresponds to the facts. On the face of it, Popper's formulations (1) and (2) are so obviously correct as to amount to nothing more than a philosopher's pedantry.

The examples that Popper offers are taken from everyday, common sense, discourse. Popper's treatment of truth consists essentially of Tarski's apparatus plus the common sense notion of truth. Now, it is clear that the commonsense notion of truth does have some kind of meaning and applicability, otherwise we would not have that notion in our language and would not, for example, be able to make the distinction between truth and lies. It is because we do have a meaningful everyday conception of truth that Popper's sentences 1 and 2, in the quotation above, seem obviously and trivially correct. The important question that raises itself here is, "is the common sense notion of truth adequate for making sense of the claim that truth is the aim of science?" In the next section I will argue that it is not.

4. Problems with the common sense notion of truth

Before raising problems for the application to science of the common sense notion of truth as correspondence to the facts, I would like to dispose of an objection to it that I regard as mistaken. If I am asked what a statement such as "the cat is on the mat" corresponds to, then unless I refuse to answer I must offer a statement in reply. I will reply "the cat is on the mat" corresponds to the cat's being on the mat. Those who support the objection I have in mind would respond to this by saying that in giving my reply I have not characterized a relationship between a statement and the world but between a statement and another statement. That this is a misguided objection can be brought out with an analogy. If I have a map of Australia and I am asked to what the map refers, then the answer is "Australia". In giving this answer I am not saying that the map refers to the word "Australia", but if I am asked what it is the map refers to, I must give a verbal reply. Neither in the case of the cat nor the map can it reasonably be said that the verbal reply involves me in the claim that, in the first case the sentence "the cat is on the mat" and in the second case the map refers to something verbal. To me at least, the claim that "the cat is on the mat" refers to the cat's being on the mat is perfectly intelligible, and from a common sense point of view at least, trivially correct.

Having disposed of a mistaken objection to the correspondence theory I would like to stress a related point. Within the correspondence theory of truth we need to be able to refer, in the metalanguage, to the sentences of a language system or theory and to the facts to which those sentences may or may not correspond. However, we can only talk of the facts a sentence is intended to refer to by use of the very same concepts that are involved in that sentence. In saying " 'the cat is on the mat' refers to the cat's being on the mat" we use the concepts "cat" and "mat" twice, once in the object language, and again in the metalanguage, to refer to the facts. The facts to which a theory refers, and to which it is meant to correspond, can only be talked of by use of the concepts of the theory itself. The facts are not accessible to us, nor can they be talked of, independently of our theories.

If theories within physics are intended to correspond to the facts, then the correspondences involved are markedly different from those apparently involved in talk about cats on mats. That this is so is clear from the central argument of Roy Bhaskar's book *A Realist Theory of Science*.[4] Bhasker's analysis shows that scientific laws and theories cannot be construed as expressing relationships between sets of events, as many empiricists would have it. Laws in science cannot be appropriately interpreted as expressing constant conjunctions of events of the form "events of type A are invariably accompanied or followed by events of type B". Bhasker's argument rests on the fact that physics involves experiment, and on the role experiment plays in physics. Experiments are performed by human agents. Human agents devise and assemble experimental set-ups, which constitute the approximately closed sytems appropriate for testing scientific laws and theories. The events that occur during the performance of an experiment, the flashes on screens, positions of pointers on scales and so on, are in one sense brought about by human agents. They would not occur if it were not for the intervention of human agents. Whilst it is the case that, in this sense, the conjunctions of events relevant to the testing of laws are brought about by humans, the laws that the experiments make it possible to test are not brought about by humans. (I can easily upset the workings of an experiment by some clumsy intervention and thereby upset the sought-for conjunction of events. In so doing I do not upset the laws of nature.) Consequently there must be a distinction between the laws of physics and the sequences of events that are typically produced in experimental activity and which constitute the evidence for those laws.

If we do think of physics as a search for the truth, then, the correspondences involved are fundamentally different from those expressed in statements about white snow and cats on mats. Roughly speaking, the laws of physics pick out certain properties or characteristics that can be attributed to objects or systems in the world (for example, mass) and express the ways in which those objects or systems tend to behave by virtue of those properties or characteristics (for example, the law of inertia). In general, systems in the world will possess other characteristics in addition to those picked out by a particular law, and will be subject to the simultaneous operation of behavioural tendencies associated with those additional characteristics. For instance, a falling leaf is at once a mechanical, hydrodynamic, chemical, biological, optical and thermal system. The laws of nature do not refer to relationships between localizable events such as cats on mats, but to something that we might call *transfactual tendencies*.

Let us take as an example Newton's first law of motion, the law that Alexander Koyré described as the explanation of the real by the impossible. Certainly no body has ever moved in a way that perfectly exemplifies that law. Nevertheless, if the law is correct, all bodies obey it, although they rarely get a chance to show it. The purpose of experimentation is to give them a chance to show it. If Newton's laws are "true" they are always "true". They are not true only under experimentally controlled conditions. If that were so we would not be justified in applying them outside of experimental conditions. If Newton's laws are true they are always true, but are usually accompanied by the simultaneous action of other tendencies. If Newton's laws correspond to anything it is to transfactual tendencies, which are very different from localized states of affairs such as cats being on mats.

So far, I have been concerned with the kinds of correspondences that might be involved in physics. Now I will consider some reason for doubting that physics can be construed as a search for the truth at all.

The kind of problem I have in mind has been highlighted by Kuhn.[5] It concerns the lack of convergence exhibited by the history of physics with respect to the kinds of things that there are and the tendencies that they possess. The history of optics provides a striking example. In the progression of optics from Newton to the present time we find that a beam of light is described, first as a stream of particles, then as a wave, and then as something that is neither a stream of particles nor a wave. How can this sequence of theories be construed as getting closer and closer to a true description of what the world is really like? This kind of problem arises, although not always in as clearcut a way, whenever there is a revolutionary advance in physics.

Another problem for the application of the correspondence theory of truth to physics involves the fact that there are often alternative and very different looking formulations of the same theory. An example is the alternative formulations of classical electromagnetic theory: one formulation in terms of electromagnetic fields occupying all of space, and the other in terms of localized charges and currents acting at a distance, the actions being expressed in the form of potentials propagated with the velocity of light. Other examples are the various formulations of classical mechanics and of quantum mechanics. It would seem that there is a strong possibility that some of these alternative formulations are equivalent, in the sense that anything that can be predicted or explained by the one can be predicted and explained by the other.[6] Equivalent alternatives of this kind, if there are such, constitute an embarrassment for defenders of the correspondence theory. Those defenders are faced with the question, for example, of whether the world really contains electromagnetic fields or propagated potentials, and are left with no means of answering the question.

A third difficulty for defenders of the correspondence theory stems from the fact that our theories are human products subject to development and change, whereas the mode of behaviour of the physical world which is the object of those theories is not. A strong version of the view that the aim of science is the truth clashes with that simple observation. From the point of view of the correspondence theory of truth, the ideal end-point of some branch of science will be the "absolute or objective truth". It will be *the* correct description of that aspect of the world that the particular branch of science is about. Apart from some minor aspects, such as the words used to denote the pre-existing features of the world, the end-point of a branch of science, the truth, will not be a social product at all. It is pre-ordained by the nature of the world before science is ever embarked on. Science, which is a social product, if it were ever to reach its end-point, so conceived, would abruptly change from being a human, social product to being something that, in one strong sense, is not a human product at all. I, for one, find this implausible to say the least.

5. Popper on approximation to the truth

An important contribution of Popper's to the project of construing science as a search for truth was his recognition of the importance of the idea of approximation to the truth. For Popper, the fallibalist, past theories that have been replaced, such as the mechanics of Galileo or Newton, are false in the light of our current theories, whilst as far as modern Einsteinian or quantum physics is concerned, we cannot know that they are true. Indeed, they are most likely false and liable to be replaced by superior theories in the future. In spite of this falsity or likely falsity of our theories, falsificationists such as Popper wish to say that science has progressed ever closer to the truth. For example, they need to be able to say that Newton's theory is closer to the truth than Galileo's, even though both are false. Popper realized that it was important for him to make sense of the idea of *approximation to the truth,* so that, for instance, it makes sense to say that Newton's theory is a better approximation to the truth than Galileo's.

Popper attempted to make sense of approximation to the truth, or *verisimilitude* as he called it, in terms of the true consequences and false consequences of a theory. If we call the class of all true consequences of a theory its truth-content, and the class of all false consequences of a theory its falsity-content, then we can say, quoting Popper,

> assuming that the truth-content and the falsity content of two theories t_1 and t_2 are comparable, we can say that t_2 is more closely similar to the truth, or corresponds better to the facts, than t_1, if and only if either
> (a) the truth-content but not the falsity-content of t_2 exceeds that of t_1
> (b) the falsity-content of t_1, but not its truth-content, exceeds that of t_2.[7]

If we go further, and assume that the size of the two classes is measurable, an assumption about which Popper is dubious, then we can say that the verisimilitude of a theory is something like the measure of its truth-content minus the measure of its falsity-content. The claim that a science approaches the truth can now be restated, "as a science progresses, the verisimilitude of its theories steadily increases".[8]

I do not think this move of Popper's enables him to overcome the objections to the application of the correspondence theory to physics discussed in the previous section. Further, I think it can be shown that Popper's view of progress as successive approximation to the truth has an instrumentalist character out of keeping with his realist aspirations.

If we consider revolutionary changes in the development of physics, then not only is the theory that is replaced as a result of the revolution inadequate in the light of the theory that replaces it, but it attributes features to the world that it does not possess. For instance, Newton's theory attributes a property "mass" to all systems or parts of systems in the world, whereas, from the point of view of Einstein's theory there is no such property. Einsteinian mass is a *relation* between a physical system and a reference frame. As we have seen, both Kuhn and Feyerabend have stressed the extent to which the mechanical world as described by Newton's theory is very different from the world as described by Einstein's theory. The outmoded and inadequate conceptions of mass, force, space and time, that are utilized in the formulation of Newtonian theory, are transmitted to all its deductive consequences. Therefore, strictly speaking, if we are talking in terms of truth and falsity, *all of those deductive consequences are false.* The truth content of Newton's theory is zero, as is the truth content of all mechanical theories prior to Einstein. The truth content of Einstein's theory itself may prove to be zero after some future scientific revolution. Viewed in this way, Popper's attempt to compare "false" theories by comparing their truth and falsity contents, and thereby to construe science as approaching the truth, breaks down.

There is a way in which Popper's conception of approach to the truth can be rendered immune to this kind of criticism. This involves interpreting theories instrumentally. If, for example, we add to the claims of Newton's theory certain practical procedures for putting it to the test, definite procedures for measuring mass, length and time, we can say that a large class of the predictions of Newtonian theory, interpreted in terms of readings on scales and clocks, and the like, will turn out to be correct within the limits of experimental accuracy. When interpreted in this way, the truth content of Newton's and other false theories will not be zero, and it may well be possible to apply Popper's conception of approximation to the truth to some series of theories within physics. However, this interpretation of Popper's theory of verisimilitude introduces an instrumentalist element that clashes with Popper's realist intentions as expressed elsewhere. It clashes, for instance, with the claim that "what we attempt in science is to describe and (as far as possible) explain reality".[9] In the next chapter I will give a strong argument to the effect that this instrumentalist retreat from realism is inadequate.

FURTHER READING

Realism and instrumentalism are discussed in K.R. Popper, "Three Views Concerning Human Knowledge", in *Conjectures and Refutations* (London: Routledge and Kegan Paul, 1969), pp.97-119; P.K. Feyerabend, "Realism and Instrumentalism", in *The Critical Approach to Science and Philosophy,* ed. M. Bunge (New York: Free Press, 1964), pp.280-308; and J.J.C. Smart, *Between Science and Philosophy* (New York: Random House, 1968). Tarski's formal paper on truth is his "The Concept of Truth in Formalised Languages", reprinted in *Logic, Semantics and Metamathematics* (London: Oxford University Press, 1956) pp.152-278. A less formal summary of his results is "The Semantic Conception of Truth and the Foundations of Semantics", *Philosophy and Phenomenological Research* 4 (1944): 341-76 and an informal account is his "Truth and Proof", *Scientific American,* June 1969. Popper's theory of verisimilitude is to be found mainly in "Truth, Rationality and the Growth of Knowledge", in *Conjectures and Refutations,* Ch. 10 and in "Two Faces of Common Sense" and "Philosophical Comments on Tarski's Theory of Truth", in *Objective Knowledge,* Ch. 2 and 9 respectively. For a discussion of some technical aspects of versimilitude by several authors, see *British Journal for the Philosophy of Science* 25 (1974): 155-88.

1. E. Rosen, *Three Copernican Treatises* (New York: Dover, 1962), p.125.
2. K.R. Popper, *Conjectures and Refutations* (London: Routledge and Kegan Paul, 1963), p.223.
3. Ibid., p.224.
4. Roy Bhaskar, *A Realist Theory of Science* (Brighton, Sussex: Harverster, 1978).
5. See Thomas Kuhn, *The Structure of Scientific Revolutions,* pp.206-7.
6. This is not the place to enter into the details of the debate over whether the examples I have given do indeed constitute equivalent alternatives. If it should transpire that there are no equivalent alternatives of the kind I have assumed, then the particular objection I am raising here would, of course, collapse.

7. K.R. Popper, *Conjectures and Refutations,* p.233.
8. Recent attempts in the literature to make the notion of verisimilitude more precise bear all the marks of a degenerating programme.
9. K.R. Popper, *Objective Knowledge,* p.40.

14

Unrepresentative realism

1. The relationship between theories and their successors

In the previous chapter I criticized instrumentalist accounts of physics and also those realist accounts that incorporate a correspondence theory of truth. The onus is on me to suggest a viable alternative. As a preliminary to that task I will, in this section, say a little more about the relationship between superseded theories and those that replace them as a consequence of a revolutionary change. It will be convenient to focus attention once again on the relationship between Newton's theory and Einstein's, a favourite example of Kuhn's and Feyerabend's for illustrating what they call incommensurability.

As I have previously stressed, the characterization of the world involved in Newton's theory is very different from that involved in Einstein's theory. In the light of Einstein's theory, Newton's theory does not correspond to the facts. Given this, what account is the realist to give of the relationship between Newton's theory and the world, and how is he to account for the fact that it was as successful as it was? In the previous chapter we encountered a number of reasons why an instrumentalist account will not do. I would like to stress the importance of Bhaskar's argument in this connection. Since more than two centuries of development of Newtonian physics involved experimentation in an essential way, it is not possible to render that physics and its partial success intelligible by construing it as an attempt to establish correlations between events, observable or otherwise.[1] Consequently, it is not acceptable for a realist to explain the relationship between Newton's theory and the world by arguing that, if Einstein's theory corresponds to the facts, then a range of observations will be in conformity with Newton's theory interpreted instrumentally. This does not do justice to Newton's theory and does not render intelligible two centuries of experimental work on it.

A related line of reasoning exerts pressure in a similar direction as follows. Acknowledging that the conceptual framework of Einstein's theory is sufficiently different from that of Newton's theory to prevent there being strictly logical relationships between them, it is nevertheless possible to argue that, if Einstein's theory is applicable to the world, then under a wide variety of circumstances Newton's theory is approximately applicable to it. For example, it can be shown, within Einstein's theory, that if the velocity of a system with respect to a set of frames of reference is small, then the value of the mass of the system will be approximately the same, whichever reference frame in the set it is evaluated with reference to. Consequently, within that set of reference frames we will not go far wrong if we treat mass as if it were a property rather than a relation. Similarly, under the same conditions it can be shown from within Einstein's theory that if we treat mass as a property then, within a particular reference frame from among the set, the sum of the product of mass and velocity for each part of the system will remain constant to a high degree of approximation. That is, from the point of view of Einstein's theory, we can show that the Newtonian law of conservation of momentum will be approximately valid provided velocities are not too great.[2]

Again, we are forced to conclude that Newton's theory cannot be adequately characterized in instrumentalist terms. On the other hand, it cannot be construed in typical realist terms either, since, from the point of view of Einstein's theory, it does not correspond to the facts.[3]

2. Unrepresentative realism

The physical world is such that Newtonian theory is approximately applicable to it under a wide variety of circumstances. The extent to which this is so can be understood in the light of Einstein's theory. The approximate validity of Newtonian theory is to be tested under experimental conditions, although, if the world such that Newton's theory is applicable to it, it will continue to be so outside of experimental situations. Newton's theory cannot be construed as corresponding to the facts but its applicability to the world must be understood in a stronger sense than is captured by instrumentalism.

I suggest that all of these comments on the status of Newton's theory must be accepted by a realist who subscribes to the correspondence theory of truth. Given this, and given the difficulties associated with the correspondence theory of truth discussed in the previous section, the path to my own position is fairly straightforward. In involves treating all physical theories in the way that the above discussion had led us to treat Newton's theory.

From the point of view I wish to defend, the physical world is such that our current physical theories are applicable to it to some degree, and, in general, to a degree that exceeds that of its predecessors in most respects.[4] The aim of physics will be to establish the limits of applicability of current theories and to develop theories that are applicable to the world to a greater degree of approximation under a wider variety of circumstances. I will call such a view as this *unrepresentative realism*.

Unrepresentative realism is *realist* in two senses. Firstly, it involves the assumption that the physical world is the way it is independently of our knowledge of it. The world is the way it is whatever individuals or groups of individuals may think about the matter. Secondly, it is realist because it involves the assumption that, to the extent that theories are applicable to the world, they are always so applicable, inside and outside of experimental situations. Physical theories do more than make claims about correlations between sets of observation statements. Unrepresentative realism is *unrepresentative* insofar as it does not incorporate a correspondence theory of truth. The unrepresentative realist does not assume that our theories describe entities in the world, such as wave functions or fields, in the way that our common sense ideas understand our language to describe cats and tables. We can appraise our theories from the point of view of the extent to which they successfully come to grips with some aspect of the world, but we cannot go further to appraise them from the point of view of the extent to which they describe the world as it really is, simply because we do not have access to the world independently of our theories in a way that would enable us to assess the adequacy of those descriptions. This clashes with our common sense notions, according to which talks of cats and tables includes what is taken as descriptions of such things. However, I would remind those defenders of the applicability of the correspondence theory of truth to physics that they, too, are obliged to render intelligible Newton's, to some extent successful, talk of light particles, and of mass conceived of as a property, Maxwell's talk of the aether and Shrodinger's talk of wave-functions.

Because it involves the rejection of truth as correspondence to the facts, unrepresentative realism avoids difficulties faced by typical realist positions. The fact that series of theories in physics, such as successive theories of light, cannot be construed as finer and finer *descriptions* of reality poses no problem. Nor does the fact that there are very different and, possibly, equivalent formulations of the same theory involving very different "pictures" of reality. Unrepresentative realism is also more compatible than standard realist views with the fact that our theories are social products subject to radical change. Our theories are a special kind of social product, although the extent to which they are able to come to grips with the physical world, which is not a social product, is not socially determined.

Unrepresentative realism is not susceptible to the standard objections to instrumentalism. It does not involve questionable use of a distinction between observational and theoretical terms. Indeed, insofar as unrepresentative realism incorporates the role of experiment as an integral part of it, a strong sense in which the empirical evidence bearing on theories is theory-dependent is built into it.[5] Successful novel predictions, which pose a problem for instrumentalism, are explicable from the point of view of unrepresentative realism. If the world is such that our physical theories are applicable to it then we will make discoveries when investigating its applicability in new domains.[6] A further argument often levelled at instrumentalism is that the latter attitude to physics is conservative and inhibits progress. It rules out potentially productive speculation about theoretical entities. Unrepresentative realism is not open to that kind of criticism. According to it, it is necessary to determine the range of applicability of theories by subjecting them to a full range of tests. What is more, it acknowledges that the range of applicability of a theory can best be ascertained in the light of a successor theory that explains it at a deeper level. In this respect it is more conducive to constant growth and development than a standpoint that sees physics as aiming at an end-point called truth. From the unrepresentative realist point of view there is no end to the development of physics. However wide-ranging our theories, and however deeply they probe into the structure of the world, there always remains the possibility of developing them at a deeper level or on wider or new fronts.

3. What is this thing called science?

My characterization of unrepresentative realism in terms of the applicability of theories to the world, or their ability to come to grips with the world, might well be objected to on the grounds that it is too vague. Part of my response to that charge is to admit that my account is vague, but to insist that this is not a weakness but a strength of my position. The ways in which we are successfully able to theorize about the world are something we have to discover and not something that we can establish in advance by philosophical argument. Galileo discovered how it is possible to come to grips with some aspects of the physical world by way of a mathematical theory of motion, Newton's theories differed from Galileo's in important respects, whilst quantum mechanics comes to grips with the world in ways that are fundamentally different from classical physics and who knows what the future has in store? Certainly not philosophers of science. Any account of the relationship between theories within physics, and the world that those theories are intended to be about, should not be such as to rule out possible future development. Consequently, a degree of vagueness is essential.

My own account of the relationship between physicals theories and the world draws on two very general features of physics since Galileo. One is that physics involves experimentation, which provides me with a basis for rejecting instrumentalism. The other is the fact that physics has experienced revolutionary changes, a factor that constitutes part of the grounds for my criticism of the application of the correspondence theory of truth to physics. More details can certainly be added if we wish to characterize two hundred years of physics more precisely. We can say that physics involves universal generalizations formulated in mathematical terms, that systems of theories form something like Lakatosian research programmes, and that their development has taken place in conformity with the objectivist account of change presented in Chapter 11. In this kind of way we can fill out an answer to the question "what is this thing called physics?" However, we cannot be sure that physics will not undergo some drastic changes in the future. It has already been noted that modern quantum mechanics differs from classical physics in fundamental respects, and it has also been suggested that the character of physics may be changing due to the social changes accompanying the growth of monopoly capitalism.

The structure of much of the argument of this book has been to develop accounts of the kind of thing that physics is and to test them by confronting them with actual physics. In the light of this, I suggest that the question that constitutes the title of this book is a misleading and presumptuous one. It presumes that there is a single category "science", and implies that various areas of knowledge, physics, biology, history, sociology and so on, either come under that category or do not. I do not know how such a general characterization of science can be established or defended. Philosophers do not have resources that enable them to legislate on the criteria that must be satisfied if an area of knowledge is to be deemed acceptable or "scientific". Each area of knowledge can be analyzed for what it is. That is, we can investigate what its aims are, which may be different from what its aims are commonly thought to be or are presented as, and we can investigate the means used to accomplish those aims and the degree of success achieved. It does not follow from this that no area of knowledge can be criticized. We can attempt to criticize any area of knowledge by criticizing its aims, by criticizing the appropriateness of the methods used for attaining those aims, by confronting it with an alternative and superior means of attaining the same aims and so on. From this point of view we do not need a general category "science" with respect to which some area of knowledge can be acclaimed as science or denigrated as non-science.

4. Relativism in perspective

Some of my remarks in the previous section have a relativist flavour. In this section I will discuss ways in which my position has a relativist character and ways in which it does not.

If we are to talk of ways in which theories are to be appraised or judged, then my position is relativist in the sense that I deny there is some absolute criterion with respect to which those judgements are to be made. In particular, there is no general category "science", and no concept of truth which is up to the task of characterizing science as a search for truth. Each area of knowledge is to be judged on its merits by investigating its aims and the extent to which it is able to fulfil them. Further, judgements concerning aims will themselves be relative to the social situation. Judgements about the aims of some abstruse branch of mathematical logic or analytic philosophy, in terms of the aesthetic pleasure it gives the participants, may carry considerable weight for some privileged class of an affluent society, but little weight for an oppressed class of a third world country. The aim of technological control over nature is of great importance in a society in which most pressing social problems necessitate an increase in technological control, and should be of lower importance in our society for which it seems that the most pressing social problems are exacerbated rather than alleviated by further advances in technological control.

This talk of *judgements* about the status of areas of knowledge decreases in significance in the light of non-relativist aspects of my position. The objectivist thrust of my own stance stresses that individuals in society are confronted by a social situation that has certain features, whether or not they like it or are aware of it, and they have at their disposal a range of means of changing the situation, whether they like it or not. Further, any action that is taken to change the situation will have consequences which depend on the objective character of the situation, and may differ markedly from the intentions of the actor. Similarly, in the domain of knowledge, individuals are confronted by an objective situation and a range of methods and theoretical raw materials at their disposal for contributing to a change in the situation. One theory may, as a matter of fact, meet certain aims better than a rival, and the judgements of individuals and groups may be wrong about the matter.

Looked at from this point of view, judgements made by individuals concerning the character and merits of theories are of less significant than is frequently assumed. My objectivist account of theory change was designed to show how the development of two hundred years of physics can be explained in a way that does not depend crucially on the methodological judgements of individuals or groups. Aims need not be analyzed in terms of the aspirations of individuals or groups. Take, for example, the aim of increasing technological control over nature. That aim has greater significance in capitalist societies than in the feudal societies they replaced. Within a capitalist economy increased technological control is a necessity, insofar as capitalists who fail to achieve it will be forced out of the market by those who do and will consequently become bankrupt. The situation was not the same in feudal society. Communities centred around neighbouring manors were not obliged by the nature of the economic system to compete in this way. A feudal community which failed to match the technological advances of its neighbour would not go broke, but would simply experience a lower standard of living than its neighbour. Such talk of aims does not involve the judgements or values of the individuals involved.

The foregoing is not meant to indicate that the judgements of individuals are of no consequence, either in the domain of theoretical change or social change. In either case, any changes that do occur will occur only as a result of the actions of individuals or groups of individuals, and the actions that individuals take will clearly be influenced by their judgements about the situation that they confront and by their own understanding of their aims. Nevertheless, what I have said does indicate that theoretical change or social change should not be understood solely, or even primarily, as coming about as a result of human judgements.

Because theories within physics at some state in its development are the way they are, and because the physical world is the way it is, those theories are able to come to grips with the world with some degree of success, whether individuals or groups judge the situation correctly or not. The fact that physics has existed and survived in Western society and has, until recently at least, progressed in the internalist way described by my objectivist account of theory change, is to be explained in terms of the relationship between the objective nature of physics and the objective nature of Western society. Part of the characterization of Western society will involve an elaboration of how people in that society typically view themselves and society, and, more specifically, will involve a characterization of typical attitudes towards physics. But considerations of typical attitudes towards physics will not be the only factors explaining the survival and development of the society, nor need those attitudes be taken as primitive and not explicable by reference to some underlying social causes.

The objectivist thrust of my remarks tells against extreme brands of relativism, according to which one theory is as good as any other, that it is all a matter of opinion or all a matter of our subjective wishes, as Feyerabend has suggested in unguarded moments. From a realist point of view, interpreted in a broad sense, the point of theories is to attempt to come to grips with some aspect of the world. This constrasts with the point of view that seems to be implicit in some relativist accounts, namely, that the point of developing theories is to convince others that one is right.

5. Why bother?

In this final section of the book it is appropriate to face up to the question of what the point of it is. Why bother to carry out investigations of the kind to be found in the foregoing pages? The importance of the question becomes highlighted once it is admitted, as I have done, that philosophy or methodology of science is of no help to scientists.

In retrospect, I suggest the most important function of my in- vestigation is to combat what might be called the *ideology of science* as it functions in our society. This ideology involves the use of the dubious concept of science and the equally dubious concept of truth that is often associated with it, usually in the defence of conservative positions. For instance, we find the kind of behaviourist psychology that encourages the treatment of people as machines and the extensive use of the results of I.Q. studies in our educational system defended in the name of science. Bodies of knowledge such as these are defended by claiming or implying that they have been acquired by means of the "scientific method" and, therefore, must have merit. It is not only the political right wing that uses the categories of science and scientific methods in this way. One frequently finds Marxists using them to defend the claim that historical materialism is a science. The general categories of science and scientific method are also used to rule out or suppress areas of study. For instance, Popper argues against Marxism and Adlerian psychology, on the grounds that they do not conform to his falsificationist methodology, whilst Lakatos appealed to his methodology of scientific research programmes to argue against Marxism, contemporary sociology, and other intellectual pollution!

As will by now be clear, my own view is that there is no timeless and universal conception of science or scientific method which can serve the purposes exemplified in the previous paragraph. We do not have the resources to arrive at and defend such notions. We cannot legitimately defend or reject items of knowledge because they do or do not conform to some ready-made criterion of scien- tificity. The going is tougher than that. If, for example, we wish to take an enlightened stand on some version of Marxism, then we will need to investigate what its aims are, the methods employed to achieve those aims, the extent to which those aims have been attain- ed, and the forces or factors that determine its development. We would then be in a position to evaluate the version of Marxism in terms of the desirability of what it aims for, the extent to which its methods enable the aims to be attained, and the interests that it serves.

Whilst one of the objectives of my book is to undermine il- legitimate uses of conceptions of science and scientific method, I also hope that it will do something to counter the extreme individualist or relativist reactions against the ideology of science. It is not the case that any view is as good as any other. If a situation is to be changed in a controlled way, whether the situation involves the state of development of some branch of knowledge or the state of development of some aspect of society, this will best be achieved by way of a grasp of the situation and a mastery of the means available for changing it. This will typically involve co-operative action. The policy of "anything goes", interpreted in a more general sense than Feyerabend probably intended, is to be resisted because of its impotence. To quote John Krige again, *anything goes . . . means that, in practice, everything stays".*

1. Insofar as instrumentalism involves the assumption that physics is to be understood as making claims about relationships between observable events, it is a special case of the position rejected here.
2. The fact that the two theories are logically incommensurable, and the fact that the meanings of terms such as mass are different in the two theories, poses no special problem for the kind of comparison of theories that I have outlined. The fact that there is a range of types of situation to which both theories are intended to be applicable (such as the solar system or the motion of charged particles in a discharge tube), is guaranteed by the way in which Einstein's theory came about as a response to problems within Newtonian theory taken in conjunction with classical electrodynamics. Establishing the interpretation of theories and ways in which they can be compared is a practical and historical problem and not a purely logical one.
3. This point concerning lack of correspondence can be made more dramatic by means of other examples. For instances, from the point of view of modern physics there is nothing in the world corresponding to Newtonian particles of light, nor to an electron conceived of as possessing individuality, a well-defined size and shape, and a location or trajectory.
4. I do not wish to make the stronger claim that a theory must prove itself to be superior to its predecessor in *all* respects. It may well be, for instance, that not all of the success of Newton's theory can be matched by quantum mechanics. Admitting this poses no special difficulties for my position, although it may well pose difficulties for those who see truth as the aim of science.
5. Section 4 of Chapter 3 is relevant here.
6. Once again, it is worth pointing out that defenders of realism incorporating the correspondence theory of truth need to explain how superseded theories, such as Newton's, were able to make successful predictions even though, strictly speaking, they do not correspond to the facts. I suspect that, in doing so, they will be forced to adopt an account similar to the one I advocate for all physical theories.

Bibliography

Louis Althusser. *For Marx.* Harmondsworth: Allen Lane, 1969.

____. *Reading Capital.* London: New Left Books, 1970.

S. Amsterdamski. *Between Science and Metaphysics.* Dordrecht: Reidel Publ. Co., 1975.

H.D. Anthony. *Science and Its Background.* London: Macmillan, 1948.

D.M. Armstrong, *Belief, Truth and Knowledge.* Cambridge: Cambridge University Press, 1973.

A.J. Ayer. *Language, Truth and Logic.* London: Gollancz, 1936.

____. *The Foundations of Empirical Knowledge.* London: Macmillan, 1955.

____. ed. *Logical Positivism.* Glencoe: Free Press, 1959.

Gaston Bachelard. *Le Nouvel Esprit Scientifique.* Paris: Presses Universitaries de France, 1934.

E. Barker. *Social Contract: Essays by Locke, Hume and Rousseau. London: Oxford University Press, 1976.*

Roy Bhaskar. A Realist Theory of Science. Brighton, Sussex: Harvester, 1975.

D. Bloor. "Two Paradigms of Scientific Knowledge?" *Science Studies 1* (1971): 101-15.

____. "Popper's Mystification of Objective Knowledge". *Science Studies* 4 (1974): 65-76.

____. *Science and Social Imagery.* London: Routledge and Kegan Paul, 1976.

British Journal for the Philosophy of Science 25 (1974): 155-88 contains a discussion of some technical aspects of verisimilitude by several authors.

Harold I. Brown. *Perception, Theory and Commitment: The New Philosophy of Science.* Chicago: University of Chicago Press, 1976.

Rudolph Carnap. *Logical Foundations of Probability.* Chicago: University of Chicago Press, 1962.

A.F. Chalmers. "Maxwell's Methodology and His Application of It to

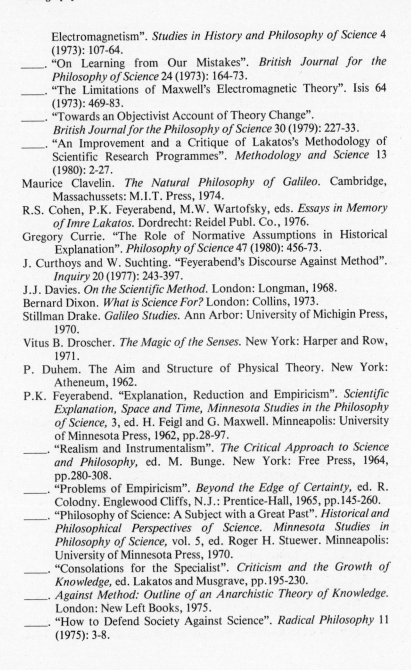

Electromagnetism". *Studies in History and Philosophy of Science* 4 (1973): 107-64.

_____. "On Learning from Our Mistakes". *British Journal for the Philosophy of Science* 24 (1973): 164-73.

_____. "The Limitations of Maxwell's Electromagnetic Theory". Isis 64 (1973): 469-83.

_____. "Towards an Objectivist Account of Theory Change". *British Journal for the Philosophy of Science* 30 (1979): 227-33.

_____. "An Improvement and a Critique of Lakatos's Methodology of Scientific Research Programmes". *Methodology and Science* 13 (1980): 2-27.

Maurice Clavelin. *The Natural Philosophy of Galileo.* Cambridge, Massachussets: M.I.T. Press, 1974.

R.S. Cohen, P.K. Feyerabend, M.W. Wartofsky, eds. *Essays in Memory of Imre Lakatos.* Dordrecht: Reidel Publ. Co., 1976.

Gregory Currie. "The Role of Normative Assumptions in Historical Explanation". *Philosophy of Science* 47 (1980): 456-73.

J. Curthoys and W. Suchting. "Feyerabend's Discourse Against Method". *Inquiry* 20 (1977): 243-397.

J.J. Davies. *On the Scientific Method.* London: Longman, 1968.

Bernard Dixon. *What is Science For?* London: Collins, 1973.

Stillman Drake. *Galileo Studies.* Ann Arbor: University of Michigin Press, 1970.

Vitus B. Droscher. *The Magic of the Senses.* New York: Harper and Row, 1971.

P. Duhem. The Aim and Structure of Physical Theory. New York: Atheneum, 1962.

P.K. Feyerabend. "Explanation, Reduction and Empiricism". *Scientific Explanation, Space and Time, Minnesota Studies in the Philosophy of Science,* 3, ed. H. Feigl and G. Maxwell. Minneapolis: University of Minnesota Press, 1962, pp.28-97.

_____. "Realism and Instrumentalism". *The Critical Approach to Science and Philosophy,* ed. M. Bunge. New York: Free Press, 1964, pp.280-308.

_____. "Problems of Empiricism". *Beyond the Edge of Certainty,* ed. R. Colodny. Englewood Cliffs, N.J.: Prentice-Hall, 1965, pp.145-260.

_____. "Philosophy of Science: A Subject with a Great Past". *Historical and Philosophical Perspectives of Science. Minnesota Studies in Philosophy of Science,* vol. 5, ed. Roger H. Stuewer. Minneapolis: University of Minnesota Press, 1970.

_____. "Consolations for the Specialist". *Criticism and the Growth of Knowledge,* ed. Lakatos and Musgrave, pp.195-230.

_____. *Against Method: Outline of an Anarchistic Theory of Knowledge.* London: New Left Books, 1975.

_____. "How to Defend Society Against Science". *Radical Philosophy* 11 (1975): 3-8.

_____. "On the Critique of Scientific Reason". Howson (1976) pp.309-39.

_____. "Changing Patterns of Reconstruction". *British Journal for the Philosophy of Science* 28 (1977): 351-82.

_____. *Science in a Free Society.* London: New Left Books, 1978.

Galileo Galilei. *Two New Sciences,* trans. Stillman Drake. Madison: University of Wisconsin Press, 1974.

J.W. Goethe. *Theory of Colours,* trans. C.L. Eastlake. Cambridge, Mass: M.I.T. Press, 1970.

Ernst Gombrich. *Art and Illusion.* New York: Pantheon, 1960.

R.L. Gregory. *Eye and Brain.* London: Weidenfeld and Nicholson, 1972.

N.R. Hanson. *Patterns of Discovery.* Cambridge: Cambridge University Press, 1958.

Carl G. Hempel, *Philosophy of Natural Science.* Englewood Cliffs, N.J.: Prentice-Hall, 1966.

Boris Hessen. "The Social and Economic Roots of Newton's 'Principia' ". *Science at the Crossroads,* ed. N.I. Bukharin et al. London: Cass, 1971, pp.149-212.

D. Hume. *Treatise on Human Nature.* London: Dent, 1939.

Colin Howson, ed. *Method and Appraisal in the Physical Sciences.* Cambridge: Cambridge University Press, 1976.

Francois Jacob. *The Logic of Life: A History of Heredity.* New York: Vintage Books, 1976.

Noretta Koertge. *"Inter-theoretic Criticism and the Growth of Science". Boston Studies in the Philosophy of Science* vol. 8, ed. R.C. Buck and R.S. Cohen. Dordrecht: Reidel Publ. Co., 1973.

_____. "Theory Change in Science". *Conceptual Change,* ed. G. Pearce and *P. Maynard. Dordrecht: Reidel Publ. Co., 1973.*

Carl R. Kordig. *The Justification of Scientific Change.* Dordrecht: Reidel Publ. Co., 1971.

A. Koyré. *Metaphysics and Measurement.* London: Chapman and Hall, 1968.

John Krige. *Science, Revolution and Discontinuity.* Brighton, Sussex: Harvester, 1980.

T.S. Kuhn. *The Copernican Revolution.* New York: Random House, 1959.

_____. "The Function of Measurement in Modern Physical Science". *Isis* 52 (1961): 161-93.

_____. "Comment (on the Relation between Science and Art)". *Comparative Studies in Society and History* 11 (1969): 403-12.

_____. "Second Thoughts on Paradigms". *The Structure of Scientific Theories,* ed. F. Suppe. Urbana: University of Illinois Press, 1973, pp.459-82.

_____. "Logic of Discovery or Psychology of Research?" *Criticism and the Growth of Knowledge,* ed. Lakatos and Musgrave, pp.1-23.

_____. "Reflection on my Critics". *Criticism and the Growth of Knowledge,* ed. Lakatos and Musgrave, pp.231-78.

Bibliography

_____. *The Structure of Scientific Revolutions.* Chicago: University of Chicago Press, 1970.

_____. *The Essential Tension: Selected Studies in Scientific Tradition and Change.* Chicago: University of Chicago Press, 1977.

I. Lakatos. "Proofs and Refutations". *British Journal for the Philosophy of Science* 14 (1963-64): 1-25, 120-39, 221-43, 296-342.

_____. "Changes in the Problem of Inductive Logic". *The Problem of Inductive Logic,* ed. I. Lakatos. Amsterdam: North Holland Publ. Co. 1968, pp.315-417, reprinted in Worrall and Currie (1978) vol. 2, pp.128-200.

_____. "History of Science and Its Rational Reconstruction". *Boston Studies in the Philosophy of Science,* vol. 8, ed. R.C. Buck and R.S. Cohen. Dordrecht: Reidel Publ. Co. 1971, pp.91-136, reprinted in Worrall and Currie (1978) vol. 1, pp.102-38.

_____. "Replies to Critics". *Boston Studies in the Philosphy of Science,* vol. 8, ed. R. Buck and R.S. Cohen. Dordrecht Reidel Publ. Co. 1971, pp.174-82.

_____. "Falsification and the Methodology of Scientific Research Programmes". *Criticism and the Growth of Knowledge,* ed. Lakatos and Musgrave, pp.91-196.

_____. "Popper on Demarcation and Induction". *The Philosophy of Karl R. Popper,* pp.241-73, reprinted in Worrall and Currie (1978) vol. 1, pp.139-67.

_____. "Science and Pseudoscience". Worrall and Currie (1978) vol. 1, pp.1-7.

_____. "Newton's Effect on Scientific Standards". Worrall and Currie (1978), vol. 1, pp.193-222.

_____. and A. Musgrave, eds. *Criticism and the Growth of Knowledge.* Cambridge: Cambridge University Press, 1974.

_____. and E. Zahar. "Why Did Copernicus's Programme Supersede Ptolemy's?" *The Copernican Achievement,* ed. R. Westman. Berkeley, Calif.: California University Press, 1975, reprinted in Worrall and Currie (1978) vol. 1, pp.168-92.

Dominique Lecourt. *Marxism and Epistemology.* London: New Left Books, 1975.

Bryan Magee. "Karl Popper: The World's Greatest Philosopher?" *Current Affairs Bulletin* 50, no. 8 (1974): 14-23.

Karl Marx. "A Contribution to the Critique of Political Economy". *Karl Marx: Selected Works,* 2 vols. Moscow: Co-operative Publishing Society, 1935.

J.C. Maxwell. "The Kinetic Theory of Gases". *Nature* 16 (1877): 245-46.

_____. "Illustration of the Dynamical Theory of Gases". *The Scientific Papers of James Clerk Maxwell,* 2 vols. ed. W.D. Niven. New York: Dover, 1965, vol. 1, pp.377-409.

_____. "Atom". *The Scientific Papers of James Clerk Maxwell,* 2 vols. ed. W.D. Niven. New York: Dover, 1965, vol. 2, pp.445-84.

P. Medawar. *Induction and Intuition in Scientific Thought.* London: Methuen, 1969.

J.S. Mill. *A System of Logic.* London: Longman, 1961.

C.W.K. Mundle. *Perception: Facts and Theories.* Oxford: Oxford University Press, 1971.

Alan E. Musgrave. "Logical versus Historical Theories of Confirmation". *British Journal for the Philosophy of Science* 25 (1974): 1-23.

____. "The Objectivism of Popper's Epistemology". *The Philosophy of Karl Popper,* ed. P.A. Schilpp, pp.560-96.

____. "Method or Madness?" Cohen, Feyerabend and Wartofsky (1976) pp.457-91.

M. Polanyi. *Knowing and Being.* London: Routledge and Kegan Paul, 1969.

____. *Personal Knowledge.* London: Routledge and Kegan Paul, 1973.

K.R. Popper. *The Logic of Scientific Discovery.* London: Hutchinson, 1968.

____. *Conjectures and Refutations.* London: Routledge and Kegan Paul, 1969.

____. *Objective Knowledge.* Oxford: Oxford University Press, 1972.

____. "Normal Science and its Dangers". Lakatos and Musgrave (1974) pp.51-58.

____. *The Open Society and Its Enemies* vol. 2. London: Routledge and Kegan Paul, 1980.

H.R. Post. "Correspondence, Invariance and Heuristics". *Studies in History and Philosophy of Science* 2 (1971): 213-55.

W.V.O. Quine. "Two Dogmas of Empiricism". *From a Logical Point of View.* New York: Harper and Row, 1961, pp.20-46.

G. Radnitzky and G. Anderson, eds. *Progress and Rationality in Science.* Dordrecht: Reidel Publ. Co., 1978.

J.R. Ravetz. *Scientific Knowledge and Its Social Problems.* Oxford: Oxford University Press, 1971.

V. Ronchi. "The Influence of the Early Development of Optics on Science and Philosophy". *Galileo: Man of Science,* ed. E. McMullin. New York: Basic Books, 1967, pp.195-206.

E. Rosen. *Three Copernican Treatises.* New York: Dover, 1959.

B. Russell. Problems of Philosophy. Oxford: Oxford University Press, 1912.

Denise Russell. "Scepticism in Recent Epistemology". *Methodology and Science* 14 (1981): 139-54.

Wesley C. Salmon. *The Foundations of Scientific Inference.* Pittsburgh: Pittsburgh University Press, 1975.

Israel Scheffler. *Science and Subjectivity.* New York: Bobbs-Merrill, 1967.

P.A. Schilpp, ed. *The Philosophy of Rudolf Carnap.* La Salle, Illinois: Open Court, 1963.

____. ed. *The Philosophy of Karl R. Popper.* La Salle, Illinois: Open Court, 1974.

Bibliography

Leslie Sklair. *Organised Knowledge*. St. Albans: Paladin, 1973.

J.J.C. Smart. *Between Science and Philosophy*. New York: Random House, 1968.

D.C. Stove. *Probability and Hume's Inductive Scepticism*. Oxford: Oxford University Press, 1973.

A. Tarski. "The Semantic Conception of Truth and the Foundations of Semantics". *Philosophy and Phenomenological Research* 4 (1944): 341-76.

____. "The Concept of Truth in Formalised Languages". *Logic, Semantics and Metamathematics*. London: Oxford University Press, 1956.

____. "Truth and Proof". *Scientific American* 220, No. 6 (1969): 63-77.

John Worrall. "Thomas Young and the 'Refutation' of Newtonian Optics: A Case-study in the Interaction of Philosophy of Science and History of Science". Howson (1976) pp.107-79.

John Worrall and Gregory Currie, eds. *Imre Lakatos, Philosophical Papers Volume 1: The Methodology of Scientific Research Programmes*. Cambridge: Cambridge University Press, 1978.

____. *Imre Lakatos, Philosophical Papers Volume 2: Mathematics, Science and Epistemology*. Cambridge: Cambridge University Press, 1978.

E. Zahar. "Why Did Einstein's Programme Supersede Lorentz's?" *British Journal for the Philosophy of Science* 24 (1973): 95-123, 223-62, reprinted in Howson (1976) pp.211-75.

J. Ziman. *Public Knowledge*. Cambridge: Cambridge University Press, 1968.

Index of Names